MW00529305

"In *Laughing at the Days to Co[...]* story of physical suffering and [...] journey not only to understand God's hand at work in it but to face the future with laughter. This book is gospel centered and hope filled. Page after page, the author directs our focus to Christ and His work for us. We all face suffering in this fallen world, but we are not without hope. In *Laughing at the Days to Come*, readers are equipped to face their own stories of suffering with joy because of our present and future hope in Christ."
—Christina Fox, author of *A Heart Set Free: A Journey to Hope Through the Psalms of Lament* and *Sufficient Hope: Gospel Meditations and Prayers for Moms*

"Tessa has two gifts for the church: a powerful, true-life story of learning to trust God's sovereignty and a unique ability to simply explain deep theological truths. I wept as I read this book. Whether you're wrestling with singleness, physical challenges, or piles of laundry, Tessa's words will reorient your heart and mind to remember the character and presence of God—and equip you to truly laugh at the days to come."
—Hayley Mullins, managing editor, Revive Our Hearts

"In a world addicted to cheap laughs that demean God and mock sufferers, here's a unique book on Christian laughter that glorifies God and lifts up sufferers. A book on laughter that will make you cry tears of sympathy, tears of joy, and tears of worship. A remarkable book by a remarkable woman with a remarkable God."
—David Murray, professor of Old Testament and practical theology, Puritan Reformed Seminary

"Tessa Thompson has written a deeply personal, profound, and practical book on how to live by faith in the midst of great trials and secret fears. This is devotional theology applied to real life at its finest. Tessa roots this book in her own experience of suffering and addresses the worst 'what-ifs' raised by our fearful hearts and answers them with the glorious 'what is': the sovereign gospel goodness of our triune God. I highly recommend this book to every believer—especially those who want a deep, biblically rooted, experiential faith that is able to 'laugh at the days to come.' As a pastor, this will be my new 'go-to' recommendation for those who struggle with anxious hearts."

—Dale Van Dyke, pastor, Harvest Orthodox Presbyterian Church, Wyoming, Michigan

"*Laughing at the Days to Come* is a biblically rich and refreshingly honest look at the realities of suffering and how the gospel empowers us to persevere in strength, courage, truth, and hope. As if she's sitting across from you with a cup of coffee, Tessa shares her personal journey of hearing loss and pain, and the fears that have come with them, and invites you to take a fresh look at how the truth of the gospel empowers us not only to have strength for today but to laugh at the days to come."

—Sarah Walton, coauthor of *Hope When It Hurts: Biblical Reflections to Help You Grasp God's Purpose in Your Suffering*

laughing
AT THE DAYS TO COME

laughing
AT THE DAYS TO COME

Facing Present Trials and
Future Uncertainties with Gospel Hope

Tessa Thompson

Reformation Heritage Books
Grand Rapids, Michigan

Laughing at the Days to Come
© 2019 by Tessa Thompson

Reformation Heritage Books
2965 Leonard St. NE
Grand Rapids, MI 49525
616–977–0889
orders@heritagebooks.org
www.heritagebooks.org

Printed in the United States of America
19 20 21 22 23 24/10 9 8 7 6 5 4 3 2 1

Library of Congress Cataloging-in-Publication Data

Names: Thompson, Tessa, author.
Title: Laughing at the days to come : facing present trials and future uncertainties with gospel hope / Tessa Thompson.
Description: Grand Rapids, Michigan : Reformation Heritage Books, 2019. | Includes bibliographical references.
Identifiers: LCCN 2019041373 (print) | LCCN 2019041374 (ebook) | ISBN 9781601787217 (paperback) | ISBN 9781601787224 (epub)
Subjects: LCSH: Consolation. | Suffering—Religious aspects—Christianity. | Hope—Religious aspects—Christianity. | Neurofibromatosis—Patients— United States—Religious life. | Thompson, Tessa. | Neurofibromatosis— Patients—United States—Biography.
Classification: LCC BV4910 .T47 2019 (print) | LCC BV4910 (ebook) | DDC 248.8/6—dc23
LC record available at https://lccn.loc.gov/2019041373
LC ebook record available at https://lccn.loc.gov/2019041374

For additional Reformed literature, request a free book list from Reformation Heritage Books at the above regular or email address.

*To my husband, Nick, whose
fear of the Lord, selfless love, and zealous
pursuit of truth daily encourage me to press
on toward the heavenly prize*

CONTENTS

ACKNOWLEDGMENTS

The desire to write *Laughing at the Days to Come* has been in my heart for a decade and a half. Several years ago, I started writing chapter 1. I'm thankful nothing came of it; the experience was there—the theology was not. As always, God's timing was better than mine. Not only did He give me a better understanding of His ways but He also gave me the gift of a sound and selfless husband to walk alongside me in the writing process. Thank you, Nicholas, for your persistent encouragement to start this project and the many, many times you cheerfully served me by giving me time to write. You listened patiently, prayed faithfully, and offered your thoughts with wisdom and graciousness. I am so thankful for you!

Thank you, Mom and Dad, for loving, supporting, and praying for me all these years and for showing me a marriage that endures through trial and loss.

Thank you, Dave and Julie, for the multiple weekends you loved on your grandsons and supported me and this project at the same time.

Thank you to the many friends and family members who prayed, spoke encouragement, asked questions, and served me in practical ways. Your love and kindness helped me persevere, and I am grateful for each of you.

Thank you, Pastor Mike Waters and Pastor Dale Van Dyke, for faithfully preaching God's word week after week. Your sound treatment of Scripture has been formative to my thinking about the truths in this book.

Thank you, Joel Beeke, Jay Collier, and Annette Gysen at Reformation Heritage Books, for the time and effort you put into bringing this project to fruition. It has been a joy to work with you, and I appreciate your shared desire to glorify God and build up His people through the written word.

Part 1

Laughter: Its Definition

Strength and dignity are her clothing,
and she laughs at the time to come.
—PROVERBS 31:25 ESV

One

HER TRIAL
He Gives and Takes Away

In the day of prosperity be joyful,
But in the day of adversity consider:
Surely God has appointed the one as well as the other,
So that man can find out nothing that will come
   after him.   —Ecclesiastes 7:14

The LORD gave, and the LORD has taken away.
                                    —Job 1:21

I was sixteen years old, and my once-bright future now appeared bleak. Due to a rare neurological disease called Neurofibromatosis Type 2 (NF2), I had begun to lose my hearing, and the loss was progressing far more quickly than I had imagined when I received the diagnosis just months earlier. When I was around nine years old, my father was diagnosed with NF2, so I had already witnessed his devastating progression of hearing loss. At the time, I was entirely unaware of the extent to which this hereditary disease would eventually affect my family and me personally. I certainly felt a degree of sympathy toward my dad as I watched him begin to navigate the world of hearing aids and isolation, but in my own near-sighted world of sleepovers and softball games, I didn't have much of a grasp on what all this meant for the future. My dad was a grown man; he could handle this, and we were all going to be just fine.

As the years passed, my naivety faded as I more fully grasped the weight of grief this uninvited hearing loss was on my father. Being born deaf has many of its own challenges; going deaf after living many years in a hearing world, however, is a completely different experience. It's impossible for the hearing person to comprehend how much the basic ability to communicate with others—whether in the intimate context of marriage or the informal grocery check-out line—affects every sphere of daily life, until that ability is taken away. One woman who went through gradual hearing loss described it well:

> The operative word for a degenerative hearing loss is always *less*, and the sounds of my world grew silent one by one. Keys stopped jingling, acorns no longer crunched underfoot, and even the footsteps themselves were finally hushed…. Conversation, even when I was included, focused on important information—never anything incidental, which wasn't worth the energy needed to comprehend it…. I considered most social events cruel and unusual punishment—not surprising when considering the effort required just to appear "normal." Even mundane occurrences such as an elevator's *ding*, bakery numbers being called, and casual comments by store clerks, flight attendants, or even toll collectors, were fraught with anxiety and dread when they couldn't be heard.[1]

As I witnessed these effects firsthand, this strange neurological disease was no longer just "something my dad was going through." Now it was something I was going through too—not so much because it was negatively affecting my relationship with my earthly father but because it was affecting my young and immature relationship with my heavenly Father. I knew that in one way or another God played a part in this suffering, and in my limited and deficient understanding of His character and ways, I wanted an explanation. Why exactly did He allow this to happen? Would He change and

---

1. Arlene Romoff, *Listening Closely: A Journey to Bilateral Hearing* (Watertown, Mass.: Imagine! Publishing, 2011), 22–24.

govern things so that this loss wouldn't get the better of us? Should I start pleading in prayer for healing for my dad? What exactly was God's place and activity in this trial, and what must I conclude about His goodness and love toward my family?

I did not have all the answers to these questions, nor did I know how to go about finding those answers. Nevertheless, at various times God did bring a measure of comfort to my soul by allowing me to catch a glimpse of how He might be using my dad's NF2 for a purpose beyond what we were able to see. I remember one particular occasion when I went on a trip to Haiti with my youth group after my freshman year of high school. We were staying at a mission home, and nearby lived a deaf woman. My family had learned some sign language years earlier in an effort to make communication with my dad easier, so I was absolutely thrilled to be able to sit and communicate with this Haitian woman. It was the highlight of my trip, and on our return I joyfully testified to my church congregation of how the Lord had used that opportunity to show me that He *was* able to work good in the midst of grief and bring purpose to this undesirable pain. For one precious moment, my gaze had been lifted heavenward where a gracious, all-knowing God must surely have some great plan to use my dad's neurological disease for His glory and my family's good.

Reality Strikes

But just a few months later, my enthusiastic expectations were met with a harsh reality when my own hearing suddenly began to diminish in the middle of the school year. Around the same time I had gone to Haiti the summer before, a routine MRI had revealed a tumor on each of my auditory nerves, showing clearly that NF2 had indeed been passed down to me. Even though there had been small indications that my hearing had changed a bit (such as my friends often having to repeat themselves), I honestly didn't think much of it when we received the diagnosis. But I will never forget the car ride home from the doctor's office with my mom. As she cried and told me it was going to be okay, I thought to myself, *Why is she so upset?*

It's not like the tumors are really affecting me yet. We already knew there was a good chance this had been passed down. After all, it had already been confirmed that my older sister had the disease as well, and she was doing just fine. My dad hadn't started losing hearing until his early forties, so surely there wasn't much to worry about for now. We'd keep an eye on things, and normal life would go on.

Normal life did *not* go on. My sophomore year of high school had, so far, been everything a sixteen-year-old girl could have hoped for—growing popularity, a not-too-serious boyfriend, endless social obligations (and the driver's license I needed to fulfill them), and just enough charming wit to keep everyone interested. And then, more quickly than I had ever imagined, those small, invisible tumors began manifesting their presence, rudely invading the lovely little world I had come to enjoy.

The occasional "What did you say?" turned into a frequent strain to hear what was being said—in the backseat of my friend's car, in the church pew on Sunday morning, during group discussions in English class, and behind the meat counter as I waited on customers at my part-time job. My self-absorbed, teenaged heart clung to every morsel of normalcy I could manage to portray. But the truth was, life had abruptly announced a new normal, and I had little choice but to adjust accordingly. This "adjusting" brought with it a flood of emotions, struggles, and tears. Perhaps most frustrating was that the nature of the hearing loss was not a matter of volume, but of word discrimination. In other words, I could hear the noise of a conversation but could not make out all the actual words being said. Needless to say, conversation became strenuous, frustrating, and exhausting. Furthermore, the hearing loss brought with it a case of frequent tinnitus—ringing in the ears that later turned into multiple sounds at fluctuating volumes.

In the second half of the school year, we took the neurologist's suggestion to go through with a weeklong radiation treatment in hope of stopping one of the tumors from growing and preventing more hearing loss. Ironically, one of the risks of the radiation was actually increased hearing loss. Nevertheless, a growing tumor on the auditory nerve can do a lot more damage than just hearing loss (as we would later find out), so in my parents' best judgment it was the right thing to do. Little did we know that just weeks later, my hearing would become noticeably worse. Gradual hearing loss can be hard to monitor. To this day I'm not even certain of the exact month or even year my hearing was completely gone. There were times of sudden decrease that were painfully obvious, however, and our spring break trip to the beach that year was one of those times. When the week was over and we returned home, a very discouraging reality stared me in the face: *this unfortunate circumstance was not going to get better, but worse.*

The rest of the school year was an agonizing attempt to stay above the water. How do you explain to people—especially the world of self-absorbed, boy-crazy, teenaged girls—that suddenly, *I need you to slow down, look me in the eye, and say it again; and can you please turn the music down because I can't hear anything above it; and can you please repeat the teacher's instructions to me because I didn't catch everything; and can you please not call me on the phone anymore; and can you please not laugh when I have to ask you to repeat yourself three times?*

I was embarrassed. Social gatherings were no longer an opportunity to flex my popularity muscles and keep up my approval ratings with quick wit and humorous side comments. Instead, communication was now one big opportunity to feel socially awkward and say something stupid. (*Am I talking way too loudly? Did I just misunderstand what she said and give a completely irrelevant answer?*) All my brain's energy was now channeled toward the difficult task of deciphering what was being said, which affected my ability to respond quickly and thoughtfully and eventually left me feeling as though I had to relearn the art of basic social interaction. I learned how to smile and nod and sometimes laugh along when I had no idea why people were laughing.

I was angry. My sixteen-year-old friends were in a world of their own and didn't understand what I was going through. So I sat in the backseat of the car, unsure of what everyone else was happily chatting about and annoyed by the music that was turned up too loud for me to decipher anything.

I was bored. Group settings turned into hours of sitting silently, surrounded by people and yet feeling entirely alone. I was no longer a participator, but a keen observer. Everything I "heard" was in condensed form, and jokes were relayed only after everyone had already laughed. I longed to be in on why so-and-so broke up or the hilarious thing that happened in yesterday's math class. And yet it wasn't just the lack of important information that created a void, but even more so the lack of countless casual and spontaneous comments that make up the complex science of everyday communication: all the little things heard (or overheard) and the accompanying responses that weave an intricate web of human interaction in which we not only come to know but are known—a tone of voice, a quick-witted sarcasm, a distinct vocabulary, a hilarious-sounding laughter.

I was embarrassed, angry, and bored, but as time went on, I also grew fearful. Perhaps worse than these present life changes was the painful reality that things were only going to get worse. Making it through high school was one thing—but what about marriage? What about motherhood? What about all the things I wanted to do that would be hindered by deafness? I remember one afternoon very clearly when I was seventeen years old. The hearing loss wasn't new to me anymore, and I was becoming more settled in that new life. But I was completely caught off guard that day when my thoughts excitedly drifted to the days to come. For a few optimistic moments I began to dream up a plan for my future, envisioning a particular ministry I wanted to start in a far-off country overseas. And then it hit me: *you'll need to be able to hear if you want to do that.* As my discouragement and worry escalated, the threat of lifelong hearing loss (or worse, complete deafness) became the lens through which I looked at the future. And to my young, imaginative self, it wasn't a pretty sight.

The trials of life make the present painful, but they often bring with them an inescapable factor that adds the weight of a thousand bricks to what already feels unbearable, and that is the factor of uncertainty—namely, *How bad is this going to get?* A previously veiled adversity suddenly materializes—the diagnosis is made, the hidden sin is confessed, the job is lost, the tragic betrayal is revealed. The crisis we never saw coming quickly becomes a part of the daily grind, and there are new and hard questions to be answered. We do our best to make it through the days and weeks, but then we begin to realize this might only be the beginning. Things could get worse, much worse. And the uncertainty of it all begs our weary minds to crumble and cower as we begin to imagine all the possibilities of what is to come.

The Lord gave, and the Lord took away. But what if He takes more? And if He does, is He the Father I thought He was?

God in My Trial

It is times like these, when our hearts are fragile, our circumstances grim, and our futures uncertain, that the enemy of our souls loves to come and plant seeds of destruction in the soil of our hearts. And unless we are vigilantly working to keep the soil pure, the remaining sin within us will jump at the chance to water those seeds. Though the Scriptures I claimed to love and believe spoke otherwise, I began to entertain the idea that God was an unkind taker and I was His target. The well-known declaration of suffering Job, humbly affirming in Job 1:21, "The LORD gave, and the LORD has taken away; blessed be the name of the LORD" was not an assertion my downcast soul could confidently echo. Oh, the Lord had indeed taken away—but if I was going to bless His name for it, I needed to know more about His character and, particularly, His countenance. Was He sympathetically looking down on me as a father who longs to comfort his injured child? Was He angry with me, and taking delight in my suffering? Was He indifferent, turning His face away because He had other things to attend to? As James Buchanan wrote, "The heart desires something more than the knowledge that it is not chance or fate that determine events, but an infinitely wise God. What is His character? We want to know. How is He disposed towards us? The heart bleeding under the stroke of affliction, or stunned by bereavement, wants to know the moral character of the Most High."[2]

What is the countenance of this God who has taken away? What truth about His character could bring calm and hope when thoughts of the future bring panic and sorrow? Of this, I was uncertain. And instead of pleading with God to help me believe whatever His word told me, even if it didn't "feel" true, I nursed many sinful thoughts and feelings toward God. This failure to know and believe who God is in the midst of my suffering neither comforted me in my present darkness nor calmed my fearful considerations of a very uncertain future.

When I think back to those first years of hearing loss as a teenager, there is one memory that will likely always remain with me. In my junior year of high school, I befriended a group of seniors who showed me much kindness. Despite my hearing loss, they accepted me and were even enthusiastic about learning sign language so they could communicate with me better. Those friendships were a sort of "stream in the desert" that year—a sweet balm of companionship that made the difficulty of hearing loss a little easier to walk through. But the loss was still there, and I'll always remember how frustrated I was that night when it proved once again to be a very real obstacle.

It was Friday night, and one girl in the group was hosting a bonfire. I had never been to her house before, and by the time I was on my way the sky was dark and it was getting hard to see the numbers on the mailboxes. I was on the right street, but I could not find the right house. I had a cell phone for emergencies, but my hearing was too bad to use it for a normal conversation. I couldn't call someone who was already there and ask for help. This was before the days of text messaging, so that wasn't an option either. I just wanted to get to the party. Even if communication would be somewhat challenging there, I knew I would have a good time with my friends. I loved feeling accepted by them. They invited me to football games, welcomed me to their table in the cafeteria, and simply made life a little more normal for a seventeen-year-old.

---

2. James Buchanan, *Comfort in Affliction* (Glasgow: Bell and Bain, 1989), 9.

After driving slowly down the road a second time, I finally decided my only option was to drive all the way home and get help from my mom. Hot tears trickled down my face as I drove. *This is not what Friday nights are supposed to be like.* Thankfully, my mom was able to call the girl hosting the party and find out exactly where her house was. Armed with clearer directions and the comfort of a mother's compassion, I got back in my car and drove to the party, this time arriving safely at my destination.

Trials can have a way of making us feel like we are driving around in the dark, uncertain of how to get to our desired destination of relief—uncertain as to whether the destination even exists. I had the right address, but there was more I needed to know. I hadn't known that the house was not visible from the road. I hadn't known to look for a stake by the gravel driveway with a light-reflecting house number on it. Once I had that information, however, I was much more confident that I would arrive at the correct house.

She who does not know God has no hope of relief in her suffering. She drives around in the dark, unable to make any sense of her pain, unable to overcome the fear as she anxiously looks ahead to a future of uncertainties. There is no one to call for help, and she is unable to find her way. But she who does know Him, even when she is in the dark, is able to run to a compassionate Father and with the psalmist cry, "Show me Your ways, O LORD; teach me Your paths" (Ps. 25:4) and "Your word is a lamp to my feet and a light to my path" (Ps. 119:105). As she comes expectantly to the light of His word, He shows her not a path free of pain, but a path full of promise. And with a gaze fixed straight ahead, she drives on, a smile of childlike trust glowing in her eyes.

Two

HER VISION
A Woman Who Laughs

For the righteous will never be moved;
   he will be remembered forever.
He is not afraid of bad news;
   his heart is firm, trusting in the LORD.
—Psalm 112:6–7 ESV

The remarkable thing about God is that when you fear God, you fear nothing else, whereas if you do not fear God, you fear everything else.
—Oswald Chambers

I can still picture that night when one of my mom's friends handed me a small piece of white paper with one short verse written on it. She was well aware of the painful season I was walking through and simply wanted to encourage me as I faced a future of uncertainty. The paper read, "Strength and dignity are her clothing, and she laughs at the time to come," which is the English Standard Version's translation of Proverbs 31:25. I had certainly read Proverbs 31 before and was aware of its significance, but this particular verse had never stood out to me. Trials, of course, have a wonderful way of bringing Scripture into a new light. "*She laughs at the time to come?*" I was intrigued.

In Proverbs 31 God gives us a beautiful vision of godly womanhood. This woman is virtuous, hardworking, strong, kind, generous, and, according to the ESV translation, she is laughing. What is she laughing at? She is laughing at the future: tomorrow, next year, ten years from now.

Perhaps the reason why I was so fascinated by this woman was because she had something I greatly lacked. I was not laughing when I thought about the days to come—I was crying when I thought about the days to come. My circumstances surely could have been worse (there is always a worse, isn't there?), but that didn't really matter to me at the moment. That "it could be worse" may always be true, but those words can sometimes do little to bring comfort and cheer to a heart experiencing real and sincere pain, especially when there is no apparent end in sight. Yes, things could have been worse, but that is one of the reasons I was not laughing—because things likely would get worse. The present was indeed painful, but the future seemed only to promise further heartache.

But here was something valiant. Here was a vision for a life that was thriving not only amid the challenges and frustrations of today but was also able to ponder the days to come—unknowns, changes, trials, and all—and simply laugh. And this laughter was not a doubt-filled, Sarah-like laughter of unbelief (more on that in a moment). This laughter was flowing out of a strong and wise woman who feared the Lord. This was the laughter I needed if I was going to endure a progressive neurological disease in a way that honored God. With this noble vision in mind, I pressed on.

Rejoicing, Smiling, Laughing

Proverbs 31:25 is translated a few different ways in various versions of the Bible. In the New King James Version it reads, "Strength and honor are her clothing; she shall rejoice in time to come." The New American Standard Bible reads, "Strength and dignity are her clothing, and she smiles at the future." Though the acts of rejoicing, smiling, and laughing are all loosely related, biblical scholars are in general agreement that the word here means "to laugh." The study note in *The Reformation Heritage KJV Study Bible* says of the verse,

"Literally, 'She laughs at the latter day,' an expression of her confident hope in the future."[1]

In his commentary on Proverbs, Bruce K. Waltke also says it well: "She is not only 'not afraid' (v. 21a), but she even laughs at any tide of adversity that may come (v. 25b).... Like a conqueror who derides his enemy...*so she laughs...at* her metaphorical enemy, *the coming day*...the indefinite future, with all its possible alarming prospects or circumstances."[2]

The picture of this woman laughing communicates something profound and beautiful. Indeed, her character would be noteworthy enough if she were simply said to be laughing at the present day, which certainly bears enough trouble of its own. But there is a strength in this woman that allows her to turn her thoughts even toward all the trials and unknowns to come and with a steady smile fixed on her face, let out cheerful and confident laughter. This is not a happy-go-lucky or "glass-half-full" attitude flowing out of mere positive thinking, but rather is rooted in a fear of the Lord. Nor is this laughter a naive and ignorant assumption that the future will be free of trouble and sorrow. No mature Christian woman would dare presume her fleeting earthly life to be a painless walk in the park.[3] There will be sorrows, unexpected losses, and bad news. But like the godly man who fears the Lord in Psalm 112, this woman "is not afraid of bad news; [her] heart is firm, trusting in the LORD" (v. 7 ESV).

Why is she not afraid of bad news? As one commentator puts it, "This woman has chosen her fears well. She does not fear the future (v. 21), but she has appropriately set her fear upon the living God (v. 30)! Thus, she is at peace with uncertainties."[4] As in every earthly

1. *The Reformation Heritage KJV Study Bible*, ed. Joel R. Beeke (Grand Rapids: Reformation Heritage Books, 2014), 924.

2. Bruce K. Waltke, *The Book of Proverbs: Chapters 15–31*, New International Commentary on the Old Testament (Grand Rapids: Eerdmans, 2005), 531–32.

3. I am indebted to John Piper for pointing this out in his sermon "The Beautiful Faith of Fearless Submission," Sermons, Desiring God, April 15, 2007, https://www.desiringgod.org/messages/the-beautiful-faith-of-fearless-submission.

4. John A. Kitchen, *Proverbs: A Mentor Commentary* (Fearn, Ross-shire, Scotland: Christian Focus, 2006), 720.

life, there are a host of potential circumstances this woman could set her mind on. But rather than living her life with a fearful prospect of what may be—tomorrow, next week, five years from now—she has chosen to live a life that reflects what is; namely, the present, abiding reality of God. Rather than being controlled by waves of emotion and impulsive assumptions about herself and her Creator based on her finite understanding and limited sight, she is governed by a right and prevailing conviction of who God has revealed Himself to be in His word. She knows that the circumstances of this life are constantly subject to change. Some may get worse, but some may also get better. But her unwavering hope is in the God who does not change, who does not get better or worse. In appropriate response to the God whose character and ways are permanent and eternal, her heart is fixed. She laughs not because she is convinced that a hopeless situation will change in her favor; rather, she laughs because she is convinced that heavenly realities will not change. In other words, her laughter is a reflection of her Father's laughter.

God's Laughter

The holy, sovereign God of the universe is a God who laughs. The psalmist wrote, "He who sits in the heavens shall laugh" (Ps. 2:4). Why will God laugh? Verse 2 says He will laugh because

> The kings of the earth set themselves,
> And the rulers take counsel together,
> Against the LORD and against His Anointed.

The enemies of God gather together, pridefully seeking to come up against Him with the intent to thwart Him. But in their rebel ignorance, they "plot a vain thing" (v. 1), and God laughs because the futility of their plans will be exposed and put to shame. Their hateful rage is no threat to His power and purpose.

Again the psalmist declares, "The LORD laughs at [the wicked], for He sees that his day is coming" (Ps. 37:13). God laughs because He knows that the wicked are fast approaching their end and that, in contrast, His reign is eternal and indestructible. To put it simply,

God knows the unchanging reality of who He is, and because of that He laughs at humankind's attempt to defy it.

Redeemed Laughter

In Genesis 18, we find the first occurrence in the Bible of a woman laughing. But rather than finding a holy, God-confident laughter, we find a laughter sadly tainted by sin. Sarah, Abraham's aging wife, is sitting inside her tent and overhears something seemingly absurd. The Lord and two angels had come to speak with Abraham regarding his future. In affirmation of God's earlier promise that Abraham's offspring would number more than the stars in the sky (Genesis 12–15), they tell him that within the next year, Sarah will have a son. When Sarah hears this implausible prediction, she laughs quietly to herself. Knowing full well that her body is past childbearing age, she questions, "After I have grown old, shall I have pleasure, my lord being old also?" (Gen. 18:12).

Right away, Sarah is caught red-handed: "And the LORD said to Abraham, 'Why did Sarah laugh, saying, "Shall I surely bear a child, since I am old?" Is anything too hard for the LORD? At the appointed time I will return to you, according to the time of life, and Sarah shall have a son'" (Gen. 18:13–14). Sarah's laughter had been a laughter of doubt—an unbelief in the truthfulness of God's promise and His power to perform it. And when this unbelief is exposed, she quickly denies it, hoping to cover up her wrong, "for she was afraid." But the deed has been done, and there is no hiding it. The Lord's gentle rebuke brings her to silence: "No, but you did laugh!" (v. 15).

God wasn't finished with Sarah. In a way that only a wise, gracious, and forgiving God can, He redeems her sinful laughter of unbelief and transforms it into a laughter of God-glorifying joy. Just as He promised, Sarah miraculously conceives, and a son is born to her that very year. Abraham and Sarah name him Isaac, which means "he laughs." Sarah was an old woman, and Abraham was a hundred years old. Understandably, this unthinkable birth had them bursting into joyous laughter. God had shown Sarah that He is exactly who He says He is and does exactly what He promises He will do. We can only imagine the humble look of joy on her face as she responds after Isaac's birth, "God has made me laugh, and all who hear will laugh with me" (Gen. 21:6).

God had transformed Sarah's laughter of unbelief into a laughter of belief, and the writer of Hebrews leaves us with this beautiful description of her: "By faith Sarah herself also received strength to conceive seed, and she bore a child when she was past the age, because she judged Him faithful who had promised" (Heb. 11:11). God's final word on Sarah is that she believed and considered the God who had promised something seemingly impossible to be faithful to His word.

In the remains of our sinful flesh, we are prone, like Sarah, to laugh the laugh of doubt and unbelief. But because unbelief and erroneous ideas about God are sinful and do not please or glorify Him, He graciously exposes them. And when we confess and repent of our wrong thinking, God transforms our unbelief into a content, biblical, and cheerful assurance of things hoped for—the laugh of faith.

A Valiant Vision

The modern technology-infused society we live in evidences that we like to know exactly what's coming next. We don't want a general weather forecast for the entire day, but a frequently updated hourly forecast. Whereas we used to rely on simple green freeway signs that showed the number of miles until the next major cities, we now have GPS devices on our phones telling us exactly how many minutes it will take to get to our destination while also showing us high-traffic spots where the driving will be slow going. And if that isn't enough, the US Postal Service now will send people an email previewing what will be in their mailbox later that day. I don't think it is much of a stretch to say that we would rather life be predictable than uncertain. Nevertheless, technology's ability to make life predictable can go only so far, and there will always be plenty of question marks floating around, many of which cause us to start worrying.

Women, perhaps more than men, tend to be worriers. We worry about trivial things and not-so-trivial things. *Is my outfit appropriate for the event? Will my sixteen-year-old be safe at the wheel? Will my son grow out of his social weaknesses? Did I make enough food for the dinner party? Will my children grow up to profess faith in Christ?* And that is why this valiant vision of a laughter-filled, God-fearing woman is so beautifully convicting and inspiring to us. We know we are prone to endless anxiety and cares, and yet we desire to glorify God by overcoming those burdens with steadfast trust in the Lord and an unwavering confidence in His word.

But we also live in a feminist, follow-your-dreams, do-it-yourself culture that tells us to conquer weakness and pursue the ideal, all while relying on the fictitious power of self. And though we as Christian women may reject these worldly concepts, they can all too easily begin to infiltrate our thoughts, actions, and motives when we find ourselves in fear-provoking, happiness-interrupting circumstances:

This will not cripple me. Just watch, I am going to beat this!

I know just how to fix this problem, and I am fully convinced my knowledge will alter this circumstance.

Surely this is not the will of God, and I am going to pray until I see a change.

Without my realizing it, some of these self-reliant notions began to seep into my thoughts and attitudes toward my physical suffering. By the time I was in my early twenties, my hearing had completely vanished. It was hard to tell exactly when it was entirely gone, but I knew for certain one day when I was sitting outside eating lunch with my mom. An ambulance went by behind me, and I didn't even know it. That settled it—there was nothing left to hear except the steady and bothersome buzz of tinnitus.

On the one hand, I desired to be at peace with this hardship and simply step back and watch God use it for whatever good purposes He had in mind. I had already witnessed some of the ways He had used it for my growth and sanctification. The hearing loss itself had confronted my pride and caused me to pull away from many social scenes and worldly conversations that would have otherwise left me feeling the guilt of compromise—something I had felt often as a teenager who desired to please the Lord but also desired to be accepted by my peers. And the pain of the loss raised my relationship with God to a height I hadn't before experienced. Though I didn't understand His ways and still had certain misconceptions, I knew deep down He was the only one able to hold me up, and running from Him would be to my hurt.

On the other hand, there was a lingering discontent toward my deafness, and through the years I became more and more convinced that it was God's will to heal me and restore my hearing. My confidence was partly because wherever I went, there was someone (or multiple people) who after hearing my story became absolutely certain that God wanted to heal me. This went on for several years, and I reasoned that God must be putting all these people in my path to bolster my faith that He would indeed do this great miracle. Many people prayed fervently with and for me, but not one of them had the joy of seeing their prayers answered. Despite this, I reached the point where I too was entirely convinced that it was God's desire and plan to heal me and that it was just a matter of time before I would have one of the most incredible experiences a person could have—at some moment, my silent world would suddenly be filled once again with glorious sound.

During this season of constant anticipation, I continued to keep Proverbs 31:25 in mind. I still loved that valiant vision of a woman laughing at her future and hoped that God was making me more like her. I was laughing, after all.

The problem was, my laughter was more self-confident than it was God-confident. Rather than my laughter being rooted in a fear of the Lord and a sound understanding of His character and ways, it was more a laughter that was rooted in my own vision for what *I just knew* was going to happen and my ability to importunately pray until it came about. I wasn't laughing because I knew God would be a kind and faithful comforter and father even if my neurological disease only ended up getting worse in the future; I was laughing because it was not going to get worse—no way! I was utterly convinced of this definite outcome, and while there were aspects of my expectation that did reflect a sincere hope in the power of God, there was also a sinful satisfaction in my own strength and faith. My joyful expectation, belief in God's power, and pleading prayers did not cease—how could God say no to such a faith-filled daughter?

But He did say no. The healing I had envisioned countless times never came.

Having articulated the sovereign dominion and power of the God who laughs at His enemies, the psalmist concludes, "Blessed are all those who put their trust in Him" (Ps. 2:12). In other words, happy—rejoicing, *laughing*—are those not who vainly put their trust in their own strength or prayers but who find themselves securely resting in the arms of the reigning King, who has the power to sustain and protect His beloved even in the midst of life's harshest trials. Their joy and peace come not from an imagined ability to change or manipulate their own circumstances but from knowing that they serve a wise, holy, unchanging God who sits in the heavens and does whatever He pleases (Ps. 115:3).

Rather than humbly bowing to this God, I clung to my expectations and my prayers and continued to laugh in the face of the humiliating and life-altering disease that I refused to spend the rest of my life with. "But our God is in heaven; He does whatever He pleases" (Ps. 115:3). I was not prepared to reconcile with that truth, and in the end, my trust in my own laughter was met with a bewildering disappointment that nearly caused me to stop laughing altogether.

Three

HER REALITY
Living in a Vale of Tears

He will swallow up death forever,
And the Lord GOD will wipe away tears from all faces;
The rebuke of His people
He will take away from all the earth;
For the LORD has spoken.

—Isaiah 25:8

Any sorrow or trial may be borne, I believe—if men only have a hope of an end. All the sorrows of this world will be cheerfully borne, and we shall work on with a light heart, if we thoroughly believe that Christ is coming again without sin unto salvation.

—J. C. Ryle, "Looking Unto Jesus!"

In the months leading up to my wedding day, I often imagined how amazing it would be if God's chosen moment to heal me would be when I walked down the aisle toward my soon-to-be-husband, Nick. When I was twenty-five, God had, in His kind providence, brought to me a wonderful and godly man who was praying fervently for my healing alongside me. In fact, he had probably prayed for it more than anyone else, and our mutual expectancy and unremitting prayers were a part of what defined our relationship. What a sweet reward to our labors if God would grant our request and open my ears on the day we were married. Our friends and family would already be there to celebrate!

But the day came and went. I walked down the aisle in silence, and during the ceremony we worshiped the God who, once again, had chosen to say no.

Those first months of marriage were a difficult mixture of emotions. I was thrilled to be married and could not but acknowledge that God had given me a precious gift indeed. But I had been so sure that part of the gift was going to be restored hearing, and when it continued to be absent, I couldn't help feeling as though things were incomplete—like I had won a fabulous prize package but on opening it discovered that half of it was missing. Life began to feel like an anticlimax, and despite the joys and fulfillment that marriage brought, a huge wave of disappointment came over me, and I didn't know how to respond to it.

As I looked to the days ahead, I no longer envisioned the day I would hear again as I sadly reckoned with the reality that such a day may never come. The question changed from a matter of *when* to a matter of *why*. It seemed increasingly clear that God's answer was no, so the question of when God would heal me slowly became irrelevant, and the burning question was now, Why *didn't* God heal me? My misguided theology did not have a comforting answer, and the unresolved question lingered over me like a dark and depressing cloud while all my hope for change dispelled. What had happened to that vibrant faith, those valiant prayers, that hope-filled outlook on the future? What had happened to that fearless woman who laughed in the face of her adversity and tirelessly brought her pleas before the throne of the Healer? Simply put, things did not go as expected.

What was there to laugh about now? As the months went by, the effects of my neurological disease actually began to get worse. A nerve pain in my leg, which had started out as minimal and occasional years earlier, became more painful and frequent, sometimes keeping me up at night. Additionally, the slight facial paralysis resulting from a neurosurgery I had had during high school suddenly worsened a few months after Nick and I celebrated our first anniversary, disfiguring my smile and making it difficult to chew food properly. The hearing loss and tinnitus were still difficult, at certain times more than others, but they had become a part of daily life and I knew how to deal with them. The nerve pain in my leg and the humiliation caused by the facial paralysis, however, brought with them a fresh and uninvited reminder that my health's future was not in my hands and may end up being a lot harder to navigate than I had once expected.

Even before we celebrated that first anniversary, the wonderful (and somewhat terrifying) world of motherhood got thrown into the mix. Our son Canon was born plump and healthy, and our hearts were full with a love and delight we had never before experienced. Looking back on those days, I see how kind God was to us in the timing of that first leap into parenthood. The reality of our unanswered prayers for healing was forcing us to grapple with some significant questions regarding the character and ways of God. As I settled into stay-at-home life with a newborn, Nick continued to diligently search the Scriptures, pray for wisdom, and read all kinds of books I never before knew existed. I was thankful for his sincere desire to know the truth and lead his family accordingly. The conclusions he was approaching, however, began to put a strain on many of our closest friendships as he became more and more convinced of the importance of doctrines that had been rather "off limits" in our circle. The gradual loss of those friendships was quite painful, but the unprecedented joys of motherhood and all the laughter that came with those first weeks of parenting (like when we woke up the day after Canon was born and realized we hadn't bought one pack of wipes) were a sweet respite from the discouragements that otherwise surrounded us.

But the newness eventually wore off, and I soon learned that like many of life's great opportunities, motherhood is a host of both big and small responsibilities that demanded more time, energy, prayer, self-denial, and perseverance than I could ever possibly give apart from the grace of God. We were now responsible for the daunting task of raising our son up in the "training and admonition of the Lord" (Eph. 6:4). I would need to learn how to communicate with him without hearing, and down the road we would also need to start routine MRIs to check for signs of NF2, since there was a 50 percent chance he had it. And in the progressively godless society he would grow up in, we would need to prepare him to walk out a life of biblical masculinity, wisdom, and fearless adherence to God's word.

These intimidating tasks alone were enough to produce fearful and overwhelming thoughts about the future. But as significant as they were, there were also all the countless everyday-life responsibilities, unknowns, and possibilities that can quickly cause a tired mother to fear even the prospect of tomorrow's to-do list. Motherhood was now something that threatened to intensify life's fears, letdowns, and uncertainties rather than relieve them. As a whole, it appeared that the older I got, the more beautiful—and yet bewildering—life became. Adulthood, marriage, and motherhood had brought with them a world of both delightful changes and daunting challenges; with the increase of many joys came the increase of many potential sorrows and discouragements. There was an ongoing desire and duty to be a God-fearing, virtuous woman whose life was marked by a faith that laughs, no matter what the days, months, and years brought. But if the cares of earthly life would only be escalating for the rest of my days, how would I ever attain to that?

Our Fearful Reality

As I have already said, women tend to be worriers. And while *worry* may sound a little more innocent than *fear*, there is not much difference between the two. Motherhood is by no means the sole reason why women are burdened with innumerable fears, anxieties, and overwhelming emotions. A single woman may be crippled with fear as she faces the prospect of many more years—or even an entire life—of singleness. A widow may be overwhelmed and frightened at the thought of aging alone. A pregnant mother may be overcome with worry in the days between every doctor appointment, wondering if her baby's heart has stopped beating. A young mother may feel overwhelmed and fearful as she ponders the unknown future of her child with special needs. A college graduate may feel anxious and intimidated as she thinks about all the significant decisions she'll need to make in the upcoming future. An aging woman may feel fearful as she notices the increasing health issues that come up, wondering if she will face a future beset with debilitating disease or chronic pain. A seasoned mother may be gripped with fear as she wonders if her rebellious, hard-hearted teenaged son will ever bow his knee to Christ.

Indeed, the sinful nature has countless opportunities to manifest itself through the vices of fear, worry, and anxiety during the course of this fleeting earthly life. As the cares of life in a fallen world pile up, we wonder not only how we will get through today but how we will get through tomorrow. And the longer we live, the more we realize there will never be a day this side of heaven when life is free of trials, pain, and perplexity.

Do Not Be Afraid

I'm reminded of what my pastor recently told us during a sermon: God never says in His word, "Don't cry." Rather, He says, "Do not be afraid." There is no reason for us to think that life in a world tainted by sin—our own sin and the sin of others—would be free from the tears of grief. In Romans 8, Paul reminds us that we live in a world "subjected to futility" (v. 20). Though believers are united to Christ and on their way to their heavenly home, they are yet in the "bondage of corruption" (v. 21) as long as they live on earth. Thus we "groan within ourselves" (v. 23), eagerly anticipating a day when our lives are no longer tainted by sin and its many effects. Revelation 21:4 says that at the coming of the new heavens and the new earth, God will wipe away every tear from our eyes, and all crying will cease. For a thousand different reasons, this earthly life is full of tears. But a tear-filled life does not have to be a life crippled by fear. In a time of great distress, David wrote,

> You number my wanderings;
> Put my tears into Your bottle;
> Are they not in Your book? (Ps. 56:8)

The grief David has faced is very real, and he has unashamedly shed many tears. But what does David go on to say?

> In God I have put my trust;
> I will not be afraid.
> What can man do to me? (v. 11)

David grieved, but in the midst of his grief he remembered his God, and his sorrow did not cripple him. The reality of a trustworthy God gets the final word rather than the sorrowful reality of David's circumstances, which could have easily caused him to succumb to fear and anxiety.

Another touching image in the Bible of life's tearful realities is found in Mark 9. The father of a child who is possessed by an unclean spirit comes to Jesus for help. No doubt this man has faced many days of tears as he has watched his son's life be ravaged by evil. He believes Jesus can help him, but he also knows there is still a shred of unbelief in his heart. And when Jesus tells him that anything is possible for one who believes, "immediately the father of the child cried out and said *with tears*, 'Lord, I believe; help my unbelief!'" (Mark 9:24, emphasis added). With the tears of his life's greatest sorrow trickling down his face, this man cries out to the God who alone can give him the fear-conquering, Christ-trusting confidence he needs.

Finally, the apostle Paul is a striking example of a life filled with sorrow, tears, and trials, yet he was emboldened to valiantly trust the Lord and not yield to the many fears and anxieties that surely sought to overcome him. In Acts 20, he is gathered with the Ephesian elders, knowing that it is probably the last time he will see them. Desiring to impress a final exhortation on their hearts, he says, "You know, from the first day that I came to Asia, in what manner I always lived among you, serving the Lord with all humility, with many tears and trials which happened to me by the plotting of the Jews" (vv. 18–19). Paul's service among them (and no doubt, in other cities as well), was filled not only with physical adversity such as beatings, hunger, and sleepless nights (2 Cor. 11:24–27) but also "what comes upon me daily: my deep concern for all the churches" (v. 28). Like a compassionate father whose heart aches for the spiritual formation and stability of his wayward children, Paul's longing for the purity and growth of his spiritual children in the many churches he had visited often brought him to tears. On top of all the pain and discomfort he had endured in his own body, he had also shed many tears on behalf of both ignorant unbelievers (Rom. 9:2–3) and childish, errant believers (2 Cor. 2:4).

But note the way Paul concludes his farewell address to the Ephesian elders:

> And see, now I go bound in the spirit to Jerusalem, not knowing the things that will happen to me there, except that the Holy Spirit testifies in every city, saying that chains and tribulations await me. But none of these things move me; nor do I count my life dear to myself, so that I may finish my race with joy, and the ministry which I received from the Lord Jesus, to testify to the gospel of the grace of God. (Acts 20:22–24)

As Paul looks ahead to the future, he doesn't know the details of what will happen, but he does know it will be filled with further trials—even imprisonment. Rather than being distraught with fear at the thought of this, Paul is ready to confidently walk into those coming days of great affliction, even expecting a joy-filled finish.

A life of great suffering, cruel affliction, constant discomfort, and fatherly tears—but not a life of fear. Not a life of anxious and burdensome thoughts about the days to come. Not a daily hopelessness and despair that bring spiritual weakness and defeat.

For many of us, however, this is not our daily reality. We are sorrowful, *but we are also fearful.* The present trials that bring tears today beckon us to ponder future possibilities that are even worse. And with each passing year, life brings about new opportunities for this fear to disable us. Indeed, the fear, anxiety, and similar emotions are often a great trial in themselves.

New and Bigger Fears

Back when I was in high school, the prevailing fear was that my hearing loss might hinder me from desires such as marriage, motherhood, and ministry. *How will I meet my husband? What man will want to marry someone who is hard of hearing or even deaf? How will I communicate with the people I want to reach out to? Will I be able to hear my babies cry?* Looking back on those fears nearly two decades later, they almost sound trivial to me now. God did fulfill those desires of marriage and motherhood, but they only brought with them new (and seemingly more justifiable) fears.

For example, now that my hearing is completely gone, my greatest fear is severe loss of sight or total blindness. Learning to function without hearing was doable, but my eyes are precious to me because they are also my ears. But since the facial paralysis causes them to not close all the way, there is a greater risk of eventual damage. How would I ever fulfill my life calling as a wife and mother (and one day, Lord willing, a grandma) if I was without both hearing and sight? Another thing I sometimes fear is long life. That may sound ridiculous, but anyone with chronic pain would understand that fear. *How many agonizing days will I have to endure the pain?* Presently, my nerve pain is probably not frequent enough to be classified as chronic pain. But in light of how much it has worsened in the last five years, the thought of bearing it for fifty more years—while it possibly spreads or intensifies—makes me anxious.

And then there is the fear that one day I will have to watch one or both of my sons go through hearing loss and all the other devastating effects of NF2. How might it negatively affect their relationship with God, as it did mine? Will their teens or twenties be filled with neurologist appointments, surgeries, and depression? Will I be strong enough spiritually to help them walk through that?

Whether we are single or married, young mothers or empty nesters, there are situations in life that, if they turn out the way we allow ourselves to envision them turning out, we fear would be the end of us:

What if my marriage never takes a turn for the better and never again brings me joy?

What if my family's history of cancer becomes a reality in my own body, and I die before I am able to see my children grow up?

What if my wayward son passes away before he repents and makes things right with the Lord? How could I ever handle the grief and feelings of failure?

What if my husband falls prey to his fleshly weaknesses and I become a victim of adultery, as many other godly women unexpectedly have?

What if I or my husband cannot find a better job, and life never feels financially stable?

These and so many more are real fears we face during the short time we spend on earth. And if we are honest, we would acknowledge that it is not only these "bigger" tragedies we often live in fear of but often many smaller predicaments. Sometimes, tomorrow's to-do list, the mountain of laundry, or the sight of the filled-up calendar on the kitchen wall makes us fearful. Winter rolls around, and we anxiously anticipate doctor appointments and children throwing up in the middle of the night. We notice the various spots on our skin and how hard it has become to maintain the same figure we had ten years ago, and we fear the effect aging will have on our physical appearance. We fear difficult or awkward social situations, wondering if we'll say the right things and whether others will rightly perceive us. The larger, more intimidating trials of life come and go in their appointed seasons, but even when there is not presently a tragic or life-changing hardship upon us, these ordinary, day-to-day cares are often enough to keep us from a laughter-filled life. And so we read of this valiant woman in Proverbs 31, and though we greatly esteem the joyful fearlessness she displays, we often do not see it in our own lives.

If both small, daily stresses and great, devastating afflictions are the reality of life in a fallen and sinful world, how might we ever attain to such a God-glorifying, fear-defeating existence? What if, when we look to the days to come, it is quite clear that relief is nowhere in sight and our trouble is far from temporary?

In Light of Eternity

Note Charles Bridges's explanation of the woman who laughs at the days to come:

> *Strength is the clothing of her inner man.* Christian courage and resolution lift her up above appalling difficulties.... *She rejoices*, not only in her present happiness, but *in time to come.* Having been so wisely provident for the morrow, she is not overburdened with its cares. Having lived in *the fear of God*, and honoured her God with the fruits of righteousness, there is sunshine in her hour of trial, "in the valley of the shadow of death," in the unclouded day of eternity.[1]

The answer lies in how far we expand our vision when we define "the days to come." The highest hope of the laughter-filled woman who fears the Lord is not ultimately in the earthly days ahead, but in "the unclouded day of eternity," where the final reality of all her hopes will be consummated.

There are many, many promises and truths in Scripture that give us hope and comfort as we think on our earthly future:

- Matthew 6:33 promises us that if we seek first God's kingdom, He will take care of our everyday needs, such as food and clothing.

- Romans 8:28 promises us that "all things work together for good to those who love God, to those who are the called according to His purpose."

- James 1:5 promises that God will give wisdom to those who ask.

- Hebrews 13:5 promises that God will never leave us or forsake us.

---

1. Charles Bridges, *Proverbs*, Geneva Series of Commentaries (Edinburgh: Banner of Truth, 1968), 626.

- First Corinthians 10:13 promises us that God will provide a way of escape from every temptation.

- James 1:17 tells us that God does not change; He is one "with whom there is no variation or shadow of turning."

- Psalm 18:30 tells us that God's way is perfect, and "the word of the LORD is proven; He is a shield to all who trust in Him."

- Psalm 116:5 tells us that the Lord is gracious, righteous, and merciful.

All these passages and so many more are no doubt greatly comforting and encouraging to us as we walk through various trials in life. These truths are important and help us to persevere in the faith, and we need to have them on our mind and hidden in our heart.

But there is a promise that summarizes them all—and in a sense, underlies all the other promises. It's a promise that not only comforts us in the midst of our tears but finally and completely wipes away our tears for all eternity. And this promise comes to us in the clear and simple truth of the gospel: "that Christ died for our sins according to the Scriptures, and that He was buried, and that He rose again the third day according to the Scriptures" (1 Cor. 15:3–4). And because Christ conquered death, we who are His will one day "be raised incorruptible, and we shall be changed" (v. 52).

The gospel promises us that this earthly vale of tears is not the end and that our suffering here is fleeting, not final. It promises us that when we laugh at the days to come, we are laughing because of a truth that reaches far beyond the sorrows and unending perplexities of our earthly days. It promises us that one day sin—and the suffering caused by it in a billion ways—will lose its sting. The people of God will be brought into paradise, and they will be fearful of nothing because there will be nothing to fear.

And here, in the midst of life's most bitter providences, is our joy and rest: "the things which are seen are temporary" (2 Cor. 4:18). And as our tear-filled eyes look with hope on these future realities, our fears are gently rebuked.

Four

HER DILEMMA
A Peculiar Perspective on Suffering

While other worldviews lead us to sit in the midst of life's joys, foreseeing the coming sorrows, Christianity empowers its people to sit in the midst of this world's sorrows, tasting the coming joy.

—Tim Keller, *Walking with God in Pain and Suffering*

When I recently began the process of writing this book, I found myself thinking, *It would be good if God brought a new trial my way so that these truths I'm trying to articulate could be freshly tested in my own life.* No sooner had this thought gone through my mind than I thought, *But please, Lord, not my boys! Don't let anything happen to my boys!*

Countless mothers have experienced the agonizing sorrow of walking with a child through a debilitating disease, disability, or tragic accident. And many others—especially in the days before modern medicine—have experienced the incomparable pain of seeing their child's lifeless body lowered into a grave, never again to be cheered by that child's joyful laughter and heart-melting smile. Now that I am a mother, reading stories about women who have gone through this heartache pierces my heart in a way I hadn't known before having children. There are other possible trials that I feel just as intensely about, but one involving my boys is certainly near the top of the list. Yet, for His own wise reasons, God has given me two healthy boys, and thus this particular pain is not something

I am familiar with. And it is a pain I don't *ever* want to become familiar with.

Please, Father, not that *trial. How could I ever make it through that?* Isn't that just the way we tend to think about prospective suffering at times? Even if our life has been filled with various other trials—ones we once thought we would never make it through—we fearfully consider other possible and seemingly worse ordeals that could yet happen, things that would either add weight to an already burdensome affliction or bring an entirely new and unknown form of pain. And as we anxiously envision such potential pains, we don't know how we would possibly cope if *those certain things* happened.

When Suffering Gets Comfortable

In a strange sense, we can almost become comfortable in a present form of suffering that at one time felt unbearable. Though at times it still brings great sorrow or obstacles and is never completely forgotten, it simply becomes "the way things are." And when we get to that point of a contentment of sorts toward our lot in life, we begin to realize that things still seemingly worse could happen—things we perhaps had never even thought of back when other trials were only in their beginning stages.

The well-known author and founder of Joni and Friends, Joni Eareckson Tada, who became a quadriplegic at age seventeen after a tragic diving accident, describes this very thing in her wonderful book *A Place of Healing*. While writing the book, Joni was walking through a more recent trial of debilitating chronic pain, which at times was excruciating and left her wondering how she could ever go on living with it. She writes,

> Those long-ago and faraway days of pleading with God to raise me up on my feet and out of my wheelchair are behind me. Oh, I'm still in my wheelchair. But I'm happy.... Right now the big question for me is all about pain.... Frankly, if this pain weren't so chronic, so jaw splitting at times, I'd leave it alone. But just as I used to tell Him years ago when I was first injured, I find

myself once again praying, *Lord, I can't live like this for the rest of my life!*[1]

She tells the story of the time she was giving a presentation on suffering and disability in a university classroom. Several minutes into her talk, a wave of pain came over her and she wasn't sure how she would get through the entire forty-five minutes. She made it through, and finally it came time for the audience to ask questions. One person asked her why she thought God had allowed her to be paralyzed. She writes,

> I didn't want to make a scene. Didn't want the whole thing to look contrived. But what could I do but plow ahead, nearly blubbering my response? "I—I have thought about that question many times...and...I've never said this in public, but...lately I have wondered.... Well, it's like this. For decades I haven't suffered. Not *really*. Yes, I'm a quadriplegic and that's hard, but it's mostly behind me. I'm used to it. I've almost forgotten what having hands that work feels like. But with this pain, it's—it's as though God is reintroducing me to suffering, like...I'm brand new to it and have never experienced it before.[2]

Decades earlier, the entirely unexpected and agonizingly painful consequences of that diving accident ushered Joni into the most intense trial she had ever been through. She pleaded with God for healing and longed for the seemingly unbearable weight of quadriplegia to be lifted. But God did not choose to heal her physically, and slowly, ever so slowly, life in a wheelchair became normal and even filled with joy. What once appeared unendurable was now an accepted part of everyday life, and God had used her physical suffering to both sanctify her and minister to many, many people. Was her quadriplegia still difficult at times? Of course. But when she began to suffer from chronic pain, those earlier days of being "just" paralyzed were quite appealing.

---

1. Joni Eareckson Tada, *A Place of Healing: Wrestling with the Mysteries of Suffering, Pain, and God's Sovereignty* (Colorado Springs: David C Cook, 2010), 18.

2. Tada, *A Place of Healing*, 24.

Many of us can certainly relate to how Joni has come to feel about her quadriplegia. We come to the day when we look back on a trial or loss that, in the moment, we weren't sure we would survive. But by God's grace, we did make it through—feebly, perhaps, but strengthened and sanctified by it in a way that only God could accomplish.

This is how I've come to view my hearing loss. To use Joni's words, *Yes, I'm deaf, and that's hard, but it's mostly behind me. I'm used to it.* Unlike Joni, however, I don't presently feel as though I'm being "reintroduced" to suffering. I haven't really suffered for a while. Sure, there is the nerve pain in my leg, and sometimes it has me wishing for the easier days when I was "just" deaf. And there are new forms of grief that hearing loss still brings with new seasons of life, such as the painful reality that I will never be able to listen freely to my son's funny and imaginative tales. But I find myself wondering (worrying), *When is something harder going to happen? Am I on the brink of fresh suffering, more severe suffering? Is God going to touch that one thing I don't want Him to touch?*

On the other hand, you may find yourself in a different place. Like Joni, perhaps you find yourself walking through the trenches of a recent form of suffering that makes former trials seem minor in comparison. You're not asking *if* something terrible will happen, but rather, *What are you doing, God? How long is this going to last?* In other words, you are not imagining the "worse" trial because it is already happening. Maybe it keeps on happening, and when you look to the days to come, you wonder if there will ever be a day when you don't feel like suffering is God's only purpose for your life.

Some of us are wondering when the potential suffering will start and what it will entail. *What is God going to do?* Some of us are wondering what the present suffering is accomplishing and when it is going to stop. *What is God doing?* And all of us are fearful because we simply don't know the answer.

Not Left in the Dark

When it comes to suffering, our natural desire is for control. We want to choose what will happen, when it will happen, where it will happen, and how long it will last. We would also like to be filled in on the specifics of why the suffering is happening in the first place. *Is there a purpose for it that will be realized this side of heaven? Is God disciplining me for a specific sin? In what specific way is God working this for my own good?* We don't like to be in the dark—we want particular answers that will bring at least a measure of comfort and relief to our pain and confusion.

Thankfully, God does not leave us entirely in the dark. When we humbly come to His word for answers, He reveals much to us—truths that are absolute, a sovereign God whose character and ways do not change, and a heavenly purpose that stretches from the foundations of the world to eternity. James Buchanan describes this beautifully in his book *Comfort in Affliction*. Read his words carefully:

> It is out of the very darkness of our present state and our eternal prospects, that the brightness of that dawn appears which shall issue in everlasting day…so that the Christian can be "joyful in the midst of tribulation."… For, while the Bible spreads out to our view the whole scene of human life, chequered with every variety of shade, it raises our eye above it, and reveals a superhuman and spiritual System, which stretches over and comprehends every part of it,—a System founded on principles which are fixed as the incidents of human life are fluttering,— a System which overrules every event that may happen, and determines them all, however casual they may seem to be, to some great and lofty end,—a System which, although in its immensity it is incomprehensible, and, in many of its bearings, mysterious, is, nevertheless, when in any measure understood, a great and lofty System, and obscure only because of its transcendent grandeur,—which gives stability to what was before uncertain, and throws light on what was formerly dark, and imparts regularity and order to what might otherwise seem to be a world not only of vicissitude, but of chance.[3]

---

3. Buchanan, *Comfort in Affliction*, 5–6.

When we bring our desire for control and our questions of *why* to this "great and lofty System" revealed in God's word, we find principles and truths that shed much helpful light on the nature of suffering, what it accomplishes, the character of the God who allows it, and so on. For example, we can ask the questions, *Is suffering good for me? Does it have a worthy purpose that trumps my pain and surpasses my sorrow? Is suffering something I should dread or something I should desire? Is it an enemy to escape from or a friend to embrace?*

These are actually not very difficult questions to answer in light of the plain teaching of Scripture. Here is a small sampling of how God's word speaks of suffering and trials:

- "We also glory in tribulations, knowing that tribulation produces perseverance; and perseverance, character; and character, hope" (Rom. 5:3–4). *Trials are good for us because they produce perseverance, character, and hope.*

- "And we know that all things work together for good to those who love God, to those who are the called according to His purpose" (Rom. 8:28). *Trials are good for us because they are inevitably included in the "all things" that God causes to work together for good in the lives of His children.*

- "Beloved, do not think it strange concerning the fiery trial which is to try you, as though some strange thing happened to you; but rejoice to the extent that you partake of Christ's sufferings, that when His glory is revealed, you may also be glad with exceeding joy" (1 Peter 4:12–13). *Trials are good for us because they identify us with our suffering Savior.*

- "Therefore most gladly I will rather boast in my infirmities, that the power of Christ may rest upon me. Therefore I take pleasure in infirmities, in reproaches, in needs, in persecutions, in distresses, for Christ's sake. For when I am weak, then I am strong" (2 Cor. 12:9–10). *Trials are good for us because they bring glory to God by exposing our weaknesses and exalting the strength of Christ that shines through those weaknesses.*

- "My brethren, count it all joy when you fall into various trials, knowing that the testing of your faith produces patience" (James 1:2–3). *All kinds of trials are good for us because they test our profession of faith and cause us to grow in the grace of patient endurance.*

Is suffering good for us? Yes, suffering in all its various forms can, among other things, sanctify us, give us an eternal perspective, and turn our wayward hearts back to the Father who alone is able to make our suffering worthwhile. Suffering has a way of transforming us in a way that few other things can. These are simple truths within God's system, and Scripture speaks quite plainly about them.

Clay in the Hands of a Potter

But when it comes to suffering, here is the honest dilemma: the Bible lets me in on the uncomfortable fact that I am not in control of my suffering. God's great and lofty system as revealed in His word shows me the smallness of my understanding, the limitations of my knowledge, and the very sobering fact that I am a lump of clay in the hands of a potter. I may readily acknowledge the necessity of suffering for spiritual growth; I may be sincerely convinced that my suffering will be not only for God's glory but also for my own joy; I may nod my head in agreement that, *yes, this is good for me, and therefore I want to embrace this.* But then I remember that I am submitting not only to God's delegation of suffering but to His *design* of suffering—every detail of it. There is no questionnaire asking me my history, preferences, future goals, strengths, weaknesses, and so on. There is no catalog of options to comb through, where I can provide some hints to God by circling the trials that seem doable. God, as father, shepherd, potter, chooses—period. And it is to His lofty, even mysterious system I must humbly submit while steadfastly clinging to whatever truths He has chosen to reveal in His word.

He reveals to us the character of the One who ordains the suffering, the truths that define the suffering, and the final, heavenly reward after the suffering, but He does not allow us to choose exactly what it will look like and what specific earthly purposes it will accomplish.

And yet we know the goodness of the suffering and the goodness of the God who allows it, and thus we embrace it.

This is the Christian's peculiar perspective on suffering, and I say *peculiar* because it is a different perspective from that of the world. It is natural for humans to resist anything that would cause them pain and discomfort. We are creatures who tirelessly seek comfort and ease. The world may readily declare, "No pain, no gain!" But what kind of pain does the world embrace? *The pain of its own choosing.* The overweight person chooses the pain of a strict diet for the desired gain of weight loss. The Olympian athlete chooses the pain of rigorous training for the desired gain of a gold medal. The aspiring businessman chooses the pain of exhausting overtime for the desired gain of wealth. The insecure teenager chooses the pain of ditching his one loyal friend for the desired gain of popularity with the in-crowd.

When the world chooses pain for the hope of gain, it does so in submission to its own desires. If the pain becomes too costly or unbearable or the desired gain simply loses its luster, there is always the option of changing courses so as to lessen the pain or do away with it altogether. In short, people of the world seek to control their suffering. They will accept the suffering only of their choosing, and whatever doesn't correlate with their goals and desires is to be avoided. They submit to suffering insofar as it serves self and insist on the option to press "pause" at will.

This is not how we as Christians approach pain and suffering. We do believe there is gain—great gain—at the end of our suffering. And we are told over and over in Scripture to keep our eyes on that eternal gain, to hope for it, to live for it, to wait for it (e.g., 2 Cor. 4:16–18). But when it comes to the suffering, pain, and loss that we go through on the way to that final reward, we do not live in submission to our own desires and choose our suffering with the aim to serve self. Rather, we submit to the sovereign will of our Father and live with a dominating desire to see Him praised and glorified whether our earthly suffering is little or much, anticipated or one painful surprise after the other. And when we find ourselves walking through a trial that appears pointless, unprofitable, or even harsh, we don't run around in desperation looking for a way to escape it. Instead, we turn to the unchanging truths in God's word that tell us who God is and how He graciously and wisely uses the suffering of His choice to make His children holy and happy. We seek heavenly gain—oh yes! But we do so with hearts submissive to our Creator, who Himself has chosen a very specific path for each of His children to obtain that final gain.

The suffering the world chooses stops short at earthly reward, and when sight of that reward is lost, the choice to suffer ceases. The suffering the Christian submits to sets its constant gaze on a heavenly reward, even when a life of undesired and unexpected suffering makes for a weary earthly journey.

What We Do Choose

On the other hand, there is a way in which the Christian does choose. John Piper gives a helpful explanation of how Christians choose a life of God-ordained suffering:

> But then, when you stop to think about it, all of life, if it is lived earnestly by faith in the pursuit of God's glory and the salvation of others, is like the Christian who goes to the disease-ridden village. The suffering that comes is a part of the price of living where you are in obedience to the call of God. In choosing to follow Christ in the way he directs, we choose all that this path includes under his sovereign providence.... It is "chosen"—that is, we willingly take the path of obedience where the suffering befalls us, and we do not murmur against God.[4]

As I write this, suicide cases in the United States are being announced left and right, and rates are rising across the map. Many of these people are without Christ and find themselves suffering in ways they did not choose and do not desire. There is no knowledge of the gospel, no belief in God, and no hope for heaven, and thus

---

4. John Piper, *Desiring God: Meditations of a Christian Hedonist* (Sisters, Ore.: Multnomah, 1986), 215–16.

there is no gain in sight. The only foreseeable way to end their pain is to cut short their earthly days.

Christians, too, find themselves suffering in a thousand ways they did not choose and in ways they do not naturally desire. But they believe the gospel. And the gospel tells us of the God whose purpose is to justify, sanctify, and glorify a people of His own choosing for the ultimate goal of His greatest glory and their highest good. And when He sanctifies His children, suffering is often His chosen means to conform them to Christ, reveal His love, and intensify their hope for eternity.

One woman suffers the cruel murder of her child when she is persecuted for her faith and chooses not to deny Christ. One woman suffers sleepless nights and exhaustion as she tenderly cares for her elderly parent, choosing to imitate her compassionate Savior and die to her own desire for a good night's sleep. One woman suffers sleepless nights of tears and prayers as she cries out to God to intervene in the hardened heart of her grown daughter, quietly trusting that God alone is able to bring about salvation.

These women are suffering in different ways, but they are all suffering. They did not choose these particular trials, and they will not choose whatever other trials they will walk through in the future, whether they are more or less intense than their present hardships. But they chose and continue to choose a life of obedience and submission to God. They desired and continue to desire to gain Christ and live a life that proves He is worthy and beautiful and satisfying. The wise and perfect providence of God has placed them each on a unique path to glory, and each of them must choose daily to walk in obedience to God's commandments, conform their thinking to His word, and look not to what is seen but to what is unseen—that day to come in which the hope of the gospel will prove true.

If we will be women who laugh at the days to come, we must courageously acknowledge that our earthly days have already been written in a book:

> Your eyes saw my substance, being yet unformed.
> And in Your book they all were written,

The days fashioned for me,
When as yet there were none of them. (Ps. 139:16)

God has already chosen His particular means to sanctify us. Some
of these means we have already experienced, some we are experiencing now, and others await us in months and years ahead. To the
world, this is a frightening reality that flies in the face of people's
natural attempt to control their own lives. That things may get worse
(or already are worse) is hard for them to accept, but that they cannot opt out or fashion things to their own liking is simply too much
to take.

Not so for the woman who fears the Lord, for she has the great
privilege of drawing back the thick curtain of earthly suffering and
by faith casting her gaze on "the city which has foundations, whose
builder and maker is God" (Heb. 11:10). There is a work that has been
accomplished, a herald of good news that she has believed, and it
clothes her in a strength and dignity unknown to the fearful world
around her. She knows not what bitter providences await her and
all the intricate ways God will use them. But she does know this: by
God's grace she has believed Him, and by God's grace she will continue to believe, trust, and obey Him until He brings her safely home
in that unclouded day of eternity.

Part 2

Laughter: Its Doctrine

Blessed be the God and Father of our Lord Jesus Christ, who according to His abundant mercy has begotten us again to a living hope through the resurrection of Jesus Christ from the dead, to an inheritance incorruptible and undefiled and that does not fade away, reserved in heaven for you, who are kept by the power of God through faith for salvation ready to be revealed in the last time.

—1 PETER 1:3–5

And I said, "This is my anguish;
But I will remember the years of the right hand
   of the Most High."
I will remember the works of the LORD;
Surely I will remember Your wonders of old.
I will also meditate on all Your work,
And talk of Your deeds.

—PSALM 77:10–12

Five

HER NECESSITY
A Sober-Minded Suffering

> Therefore gird up the loins of your mind, be sober, and rest
> your hope fully upon the grace that is to be brought to you at
> the revelation of Jesus Christ.
>
> —1 Peter 1:13

When I was in middle school, I remember going to Friday night
sleepovers and eating all the junk food I wanted—cookies, soda,
greasy pepperoni pizza, handfuls of Skittles, and the like. In the
moment, it felt fun to overload my body with sugar and carbs (though
I don't remember ever waking up the next day feeling great). During these years I also complained regularly of having stomachaches
while at the same time having no problem eating a plate of chocolate
chip pancakes from IHOP for breakfast coupled with a big glass of
chocolate milk or pairing a cinnamon crunch bagel with a caramel
frappe when I went to my favorite café for lunch. Suffice it to say, I
was quite ignorant about how all that sugar was affecting me physically, but I was aware of the obvious fact that the number on the scale
was always higher than I wanted it to be.

The year after I graduated from high school, I read a health book
that promoted a certain diet, and it radically changed my thinking
toward food and eating. When I understood more of how the body
was supposed to work and what foods greatly hindered it from working properly, I was motivated and equipped to change my actions. The
chocolate chip pancakes and cinnamon crunch bagel were ditched in

favor of whole grains, and overall, I began to take more careful note of whether the food I was putting into my body was helping it or harming it. As I have continued to learn about nutrition over the years, the information I take in and regularly consider affects my grocery shopping trips, my order at a restaurant, the meals I serve my kids, and what I consider a treat.

I firmly believe there is a time for a cookies and cream waffle cone! The point is, because I know how my body works and what certain foods do to it—both short- and long-term—my thinking about that cookies and cream waffle cone is such that I would not choose to eat one every day. It may sound good a lot of the time, but my knowledge informs my thoughts and affections, both of which play a great part in my actions.

The things we know and believe ultimately affect the way we act. The apostle Paul certainly understood this principle because his epistles are made up of both doctrine (what the Christian needs to know) and practice (how the Christian is to live in response). He did not expect his readers to live a certain way without informing them of truths that gave them an understanding of *why* and *how* to live that way. Notice the way he prayed for the Colossians: "For this reason we also, since the day we heard it, do not cease to pray for you, and to ask that you may be filled with the knowledge of His will in all wisdom and spiritual understanding; that you may walk worthy of the Lord, fully pleasing Him, being fruitful in every good work and increasing in the knowledge of God" (Col. 1:9–10). In other words, *we pray that you will* know *so that you will* do.

One way that New Testament authors communicate this connection is by using the word *therefore*, which serves as a bridge between the truth and the action. The apostle Peter does this in the first chapter of his first epistle: "Therefore gird up the loins of your mind, be sober, and rest your hope fully upon the grace that is to be brought to you at the revelation of Jesus Christ" (v. 13). Before we consider this verse more closely, a brief look at the letter's background is helpful for understanding Peter's purpose in writing.

A Letter of Hope for a Suffering People

The book of 1 Peter has been called "the epistle of hope," and rightly so. This encouraging letter is filled with foundational gospel truths regarding the past, present, and future—truths that if rightly understood and steadfastly believed would steady the minds and hearts of its original readers, who were evidently suffering persecution for their faith (1:6–7; 2:19–20; 3:14–15; 4:14; 5:9). For the purpose at hand, we could say that 1 Peter is a book about laughing at the days to come. According to Peter, the readers had every reason to be rejoicing as they looked to the future through the lens of the gospel. In the first chapter, Peter says that God has caused them to be born again "to a living hope" (v. 3).

Peter does not want his readers to possess mere wishful thinking: *I wish the suffering would stop. I wish I knew when it would be over.* Hope is much more than wishful thinking. The 1828 edition of *Webster's Dictionary* defines *hope* as,

> A desire of some good, accompanied with at least a slight expectation of obtaining it, or a belief that it is obtainable. *Hope* differs from wish and desire in this, that it implies some expectation of obtaining the good desired, or the possibility of possessing it. *Hope* therefore always gives pleasure or joy; whereas wish and desire may produce or be accompanied with pain and anxiety.[1]

According to this definition of *hope*, to say, "I wish this suffering would end" is much different from saying, "I possess hope that this suffering will one day end." And yet even *Webster's* definition of *hope* falls short—for God's promises to us in Christ are not merely a "possibility" but an absolute certainty. And therefore we have not a "slight expectation" of obtaining them but rather a sincere, sure, and confident expectation. That is the Christian's hope and the hope

---

1. Noah Webster, "Hope," in *Noah Webster's First Edition of an American Dictionary of the English Language* (1828; repr., San Francisco: Foundation for American Christian Education, 1985).

Peter wanted his readers to possess as a result of their knowing and believing the gospel.

After reminding the readers of the hope they have in the gospel, Peter addressed the reality of their present suffering:

> In this you greatly rejoice, though now for a little while, if need be, you have been grieved by various trials, that the genuineness of your faith, being much more precious than gold that perishes, though it is tested by fire, may be found to praise, honor, and glory at the revelation of Jesus Christ, whom having not seen you love. Though now you do not see Him, *yet believing, you rejoice* with joy inexpressible and full of glory, receiving the end of your faith—the salvation of your souls. (1 Peter 1:6–9, emphasis added)

Their circumstances were difficult, yet believing, they rejoiced because the gospel tells them there is a day to come when their suffering would be over and their salvation would be complete (as Peter just reminded them in the first five verses). It also tells them of the God with whom an intimate, unbreakable union is entirely sufficient to comfort, uphold, and enable them as they walk through many weary earthly days on the way to their heavenly home.

While we don't know specific details about the nature of their persecution, it is safe to say that many of the readers were probably beginning to wonder, *How bad is this going to get? Will the persecution intensify? Is Christianity worth it?* Perhaps some of them hadn't suffered in a considerable way yet, but the stories they had been hearing were causing them to be overcome with anxiety and fear. Perhaps some of them had already been hit hard, and they were wondering whether their faith was strong enough to take another blow. Whatever the case, Peter's goal was to leave his readers filled with an unwavering hope—a *rejoicing* hope—founded on the unchanging truths of the gospel that they knew and believed.

Having laid the foundation, he then pulls out his *therefore*. In the preceding verses, Peter had been reminding his readers that this is the reality of the gospel, so "therefore, gird up the loins of your mind, be sober, and rest your hope fully upon the grace that is to be brought to you at the revelation of Jesus Christ" (1 Peter 1:13).

We don't see it as easily in our English translations, but the first two commands here are actually participles in the Greek, meaning they are subordinate to and support the main command to rest your hope on God's grace in Christ.[2] We could say it like this: "As you gird up the loins of your mind and are sober, rest your hope fully on the grace that is to be brought to you at the revelation of Jesus Christ."

Peter's main concern was that his readers would be filled with a rejoicing hope as a result of their belief in the gospel and its encouraging implications for the future. The gospel is what they needed to *know*, and hoping is what they needed to *do*—but how could they get from one to the other? How could they use their knowledge to cultivate hope? According to Peter, they cultivated hope by girding up the loins of their mind and being sober.

But I'm Not Being Persecuted!
Before we move on, I want to briefly address an objection that might arise at this point. When we learn that the original readers of 1 Peter were going through persecution for their Christian faith, we may find it difficult to relate, feeling as though the encouragement in the epistle doesn't really apply to us because our suffering is not due to persecution but simply is the result of living in a sinful and fallen world of cancer, car problems, and relational conflict. There is a tendency to put persecution on a pedestal, thinking more highly of the Christian who is imprisoned for her faith than the Christian who maintains her joy and peace as she walks through her second miscarriage. In short, we often focus more on the *cause* of the suffering than the *response* to and *outcome* of the suffering. Too much focus on the cause makes the suffering all about the sufferer. The imprisoned person is immediately praised because of her great faith, but the woman with cancer? *Well, perhaps if she had eaten better earlier*

2. Peter H. Davids, *The First Epistle of Peter*, New International Commentary on the New Testament (Grand Rapids: Eerdmans, 1990), 66.

in life, she wouldn't have gotten it, we are tempted to reason. The woman whose daughter has left the church and rejected the faith she was taught? *Well, perhaps if her mom had set a godlier example, she wouldn't have left.*

There are certainly times when God will expose our sin as we are suffering. When that happens, the obvious answer is repentance: take it to God in confession, trust in the pardoning blood of Christ, and then by God's grace turn away from that sin. The truth is, however, we are not all-knowing creatures and are not always able to determine an exact cause for every trial we face. But whether the cause of a trial is known or unknown, God can and should be glorified in the way we respond and grow as a result of it.

Therefore, we can apply the book of 1 Peter to general suffering and hard times because Peter's primary goal in his epistle is not to teach his readers about the cause of their suffering but to teach them about the necessary God-glorifying response (hope) and outcome (holiness). Their persecution certainly gives them a prime opportunity to hope, but all Christians—whether they are sick or healthy, persecuted or safe, rich or poor—are called to hope! The sleep-deprived and financially strapped mother of five young children and the woman whose husband was martyred for confessing Christ both need the encouragement of 1 Peter because they are both called to put their hope in Christ and walk in holiness. I really appreciate how John Piper puts it: "All experiences of suffering in the path of Christian obedience, whether from persecution, or sickness, or accident, have this in common: they all threaten our faith in the goodness of God and tempt us to leave the path of obedience. Therefore, every triumph of faith and all perseverance in obedience are testimonies to the goodness of God and the preciousness of Christ—whether the enemy is sickness, Satan, sin, or sabotage."[3]

---

3. Piper, *Desiring God*, 216.

Loins Girt and Minds Alert

Going back now to 1 Peter 1:13, what did Peter mean when he told his readers to "gird up the loins" of their mind? Simon Kistemaker explains, "The double metaphor *loins* and *mind* is somewhat confusing. But the picture is clear when we think of a first-century person who tucked the folds of his long, flowing garment under his belt so that he was no longer hindered in his walk or work…. Peter then applies that imagery to the mind. He is saying: 'Let nothing hinder your mind as you put it to work.'"[4]

We could also picture a bride wearing a beautiful gown with a long, flowing train. The train is entirely appropriate for the ceremony and further adorns the bride as she walks slowly down the aisle toward her groom. As the bride says her vows, the maid of honor makes it her special task to make sure the train is laid out smoothly for all to see. When it comes time for the reception, however, the bride will probably want a little more freedom to walk around without hindrance. To provide for that, many dresses now come with very small snaps or buttons and loops on the back so that the train can be adjusted for the reception, making it much easier for the bride to walk about freely as she greets her guests.

Peter was calling his readers to an expectant hope, and if they were going to hope, they needed to be thinking correctly about the sure object of their hope. Their minds could not be muddled and slowed down by errors, half-truths, and impulsive emotions. Isn't that what suffering—or the fear of suffering—does to our minds sometimes? We want (*need*) to put them to work, but our painful circumstances and the thought patterns and emotions they evoke are like a long robe dragging along in the dirt, making it hard for us to think and respond the way we ought to. Therefore, if we are to be filled with a clear-minded, biblical hope even in the midst of suffering, our minds must be ready to go, ready to both dwell on things that are true and quickly reject things that are not.

---

4. Simon J. Kistemaker, *James, Epistles of John, Peter, and Jude*, New Testament Commentary (Grand Rapids: Baker Academic, 2007), 58.

On a related note, Peter adds that we are to cultivate hope by being "sober." We naturally associate the word *sober* with the body being free from the intoxicating effects of alcohol. In the New Testament, however, being *sober* refers to having a clear mind and, as a result, sound judgment.

Paul uses this word in his first letter to the Thessalonians: "But let us who are of the day be sober, putting on the breastplate of faith and love, and as a helmet the hope of salvation" (1 Thess. 5:8). Here we see Paul making the same connection between being sober and having hope toward the future, when salvation in Christ will be fully realized.

The spiritually sober woman is earnest and alert. Her mind is uncluttered and readily able to evaluate a situation according to God's word. Her zeal and consistency are not slowed down by the cares of this world, and she is always on guard against things that will cause her to become spiritually sluggish or erroneous. When it comes to being sober, we are thinking about more than staying away from outright heresy. Yes, false doctrine—whether subtle or obvious—will "intoxicate" us spiritually, causing us to have wrong judgment and putting us on a harmful path to further error. But there are also 101 other things that can cause us to become "cloudy minded" and less vigilant in our thoughts and their resulting actions. All people, whether they are going through a time of suffering or not, have one or more areas of weakness in which they are more easily numbed to eternal realities. This could be food, television, trips to Target, social media, excessive online shopping, romance novels, and the list of distractions goes on. Sometimes we turn to these things in an effort to escape or lessen a present pain. And sometimes we turn to these things while life is going smoothly, trying to enjoy the days as much as possible since we assume trials are bound to come eventually.

The things that drain one person's spiritual alertness will be different from the things that drain another person's spiritual alertness. One thing that tends to lessen mine is excessive use of my smartphone—scrolling through the daily news (multiple times a day), browsing the new arrivals at my favorite store (when I'm not even planning to buy anything), and reverting to Google with every whim of curiosity. Is it wrong to *ever* browse the news or search Google for a recipe? Of course not—technology is a gift from God. But our minds are prone to wander, and the remaining sin in our hearts seeks to take every good and lawful gift of God and turn it into something that draws us away from the Giver. And thus there is a need for intentional watchfulness in the areas that tend to distract and consume us most easily.

On the one hand, a distracted, cloudy-minded woman whose mind and heart are set on the passing cares of this world will not be a woman who is laughing at the days to come. Such a mind will not produce a steadfast hope of heaven and a delight in the gospel truths that are getting her there. When trials come—and they will—her mind will not be ready to go. Her thoughts of God will be few, false, or fearful.

On the other hand, a woman who is watchful of what is coming into her mind and whose habits, affections, and thought patterns are increasingly governed by a knowledge of and belief in God's word will be a woman who is able to see past the present pain and set her hope on a promise—the promise of the gospel. And because her mind is daily alert and ready to think clearly, the emotions of those toughest, most tear- or worry-filled days will not get the final word. She may be afflicted in every way, but she will not be crushed. She may be perplexed, but she will not be driven to despair (2 Cor. 4:8).

Like the psalmist, we may at times find ourselves asking,

> Has [God's] promise failed forevermore?
> Has God forgotten to be gracious?
> Has He in anger shut up His tender mercies? (Ps. 77:8–9)

But if our minds are spiritually alert, we will be able to say in the next breath,

> I will remember the works of the LORD;
> Surely I will remember Your wonders of old.
> I will also meditate on all Your work,
> And talk of Your deeds. (vv. 11–12)

A Beautiful Example of Spiritual Sobriety

In her autobiography *Evidence Not Seen*, Darlene Deibler Rose tells her amazing story of living as a prisoner of war of the Japanese army during World War II. While working as a missionary in Indonesia, she was suddenly separated from her dear husband, Russell, and taken to a prison camp where food was scarce, authorities were brutal, and disease—and death—were imminent. The prospect of being freed was comforting, but because she had no contact with the world outside the prison camp, there was no way for her to know whether that prospect was realistic or entirely naive.

Having already lived through years of hunger, sickness, and exposure as a prisoner, Darlene tells of a time when her mind began to dwell on the days to come, and she began to wonder what further pain and tragedy might await her:

> Gradually I drifted into the spiritually unprofitable game of "suppose"! *Suppose* the Japanese do win the war, what then?... *Suppose* my brothers Donald and Ray are here somewhere in the South Pacific.... *Suppose* Don and Ray are killed, what of their families? What of Mother and Dad? *Suppose* none of us makes it home?
>
> There is nothing that will plunge a person into despair more quickly than to *suppose* what could happen. This was another example of the worries of tomorrow that never come, robbing us of the joys of today.... In my moment of terrible aloneness and sorrow for a world of people so devastated by war, I heard someone with a beautiful, clear voice singing "Precious Name, Oh, How Sweet" outside my cell.... My heart burst with bright hope! The "time to weep" was past; it was a "time to laugh."
>
> "O Lord," I cried, "forgive me. It isn't a game of 'suppose.' I live in the sure knowledge that 'the name of the Lord is a strong tower: the righteous runneth into it, and is safe.'"[5]

Even in her darkest hour, when she looked ahead and was unable to see anything lovely or comforting, when she saw a future

---

5. Darlene Deibler Rose, *Evidence Not Seen: A Woman's Miraculous Faith in the Jungles of World War II* (New York: HarperCollins, 2003), 152.

filled with many potential pains—even then, her mind was spiritually alert, and she immediately caught herself when she began to dwell on fearful "what-ifs." Rather than allowing herself to stay there, she quickly reminded herself of what she knew to be true: *I may not know what will happen tomorrow or next year, but I do know my Lord. I am sure of who He is, and that is enough.* Darlene's sober-minded response to her game of "suppose" caused her to evaluate her circumstances biblically, which left her not with despair but with hope and peace.

Did she shed many tears? Yes. Did her emotional and physical pain feel unbearable at times? Yes. But she did not lose heart. The testimony of her life echoes the words of Paul:

> Therefore we do not lose heart. Even though our outward man is perishing, yet the inward man is being renewed day by day. For our light affliction, which is but for a moment, is working for us a far more exceeding and eternal weight of glory, while we do not look at the things which are seen, but at the things which are not seen. For the things which are seen are temporary, but the things which are not seen are eternal. (2 Cor. 4:16–18)

When Scripture Gets Uncomfortable

As I said in the beginning of the chapter, contrary to my days of junk-food sleepovers, I try to eat with my overall health in mind and pay attention to the ingredients in the food I buy. My six-year-old likes to joke about high fructose corn syrup because he knows it's a "no-no" around here. That being said, there are admittedly times when I simply don't want to know what is in the food I'm eating because either the nutritional information or the ingredients list would make me squirm a bit. I'd rather not know how much saturated fat is in the delicious Chicago-style deep-dish pizza we eat whenever we visit my in-laws. And when it's time for my mom to make the frosting for the spice cake I request each year for my birthday, the best thing to do is to completely ignore the enormous bowl of brown sugar on the counter. These foods are not a part of my everyday diet and are eaten only on occasion, so I would rather be ignorant, enjoy them, and get back to healthier eating the next day.

When it comes to the Bible, there are certain passages that make us squirm a little. We are tempted to read them quickly without thinking or not read them at all because if they say what they seem to be saying, we would be uncomfortable and unsure of how to respond. We would rather enjoy the comfort of our favorite passages and not have to face up to the possibility of being corrected in our understanding of God.

On another note, some of us may stay away from certain passages simply because we are indifferent as to whether or not we understand them rightly. The thought of reading moderate- or beginner-level theological books is uninteresting, and listening to sermons that carefully expound and apply Scripture requires too much thought and concentration. As long as we consider ourselves saved, we are content with surface-level understanding and a pile of Christian romance novels.

I am not saying that we should read only nonfiction doctrinal books and that everything else is a waste of time. I also understand that mothers of little ones (or three athletic teenagers, for that matter) often have little time for reading anything more than the Bible. The issue isn't how much we read and study but whether or not we actually care about our understanding of the things of God. If we never have a desire to dig in to a book that would enlarge our understanding of Christ, salvation, suffering, prayer, or spiritual disciplines, why is that? Why are we satisfied with little (or wrong) thoughts about God and His word? Do we really believe that it's important for Christ-professing women to know what they believe and why they believe it? Or do we excuse ourselves with the thought, *I'm just not "that kind" of woman. I respect those women who teach the Bible studies and get excited about theology, but I just don't have it in me.*

If you find yourself with little desire to deepen your understanding of God's word or a hesitancy to let the pages of Scripture confront you in your long-held assumptions, ask God to change that. We do not expect Him to answer that prayer by making us scholars, but we can expect Him to graciously help us become students. And while few of us will ever be called to be seminary students, we are all called to be sincere students—our minds ready and willing to work that we might be increasingly correct in the way we think about God and the life we live before Him in response.

Come humbly to God's word, and if something you read makes you squirm in discomfort, don't skip over it. Read it again and pray for the grace to both understand and joyfully submit.

Fearing the Lord in Every Circumstance

Remember, the Proverbs 31 woman who laughs at the days to come is said to be a woman who fears the Lord (v. 30). Notice how John Murray describes this fear, particularly how it relates to having a mind that is sober and "girded up." He says, "The first thoughts of the godly man in every circumstance is God's relation to him and it, and his and its relation to God. That is God-consciousness and that is what the fear of God entails."[6]

When we find ourselves in a difficult circumstance (or imagining a prospective one), we often think first about how it makes us feel:

Will the loss be more than my heart can bear?

How would I be able to function if the physical pain got worse?

If that happened, it would put so much stress on the family.

This ongoing conflict is so frustrating, and I can't seem to get past the anger and bitterness I'm feeling from it.

The fear of the Lord does not throw out feelings entirely, but it does put them in their proper place. Rather than letting feelings and emotions control our perspective and judgment in difficult circumstances, the fear of the Lord causes our perspective to be molded by the question, Who is God in this? which is then followed by the question, Who am I in this? The God-fearing woman, with the loins

6. John Murray, *Principles of Conduct: Aspects of Biblical Ethics* (Grand Rapids: Eerdmans, 1984), 238.

of her mind girded up, will then turn her thoughts toward God's word and answer truthfully in light of what she knows to be true about God and herself—even when those truths are sometimes hard to swallow.

If we would be honest, most of us would probably have to admit that we are often without this "God-consciousness" as we go about a typical day. Joyful and affectionate thoughts of God's fatherly sovereignty, Christ's selfless and submissive suffering, and the Holy Spirit's sanctifying power may surface during a sermon I hear on Sunday, but they are seldom found by Tuesday afternoon when the doctor calls with the test results, the nerve pain returns, and the kids are revealing once again just how badly they're in need of a Savior.

If someone were to ask us what a Christian is, we could explain the basics. If we were asked to write out a personal testimony of how we came to faith in Christ, we would likely think back to a time when we were deeply convicted of our sin and were given to put all our trust for salvation in Christ alone and what He accomplished on the cross, and then go on to testify of how our coming to know God has made a difference in our lives. And if we found ourselves sitting through a funeral service, whether for a believer or nonbeliever, then too would our thoughts likely turn toward the weighty, eternal realities of the gospel that have now been realized by the departed soul—either the immense joy and consolation of eternity with Christ or the inconceivable devastation that comes to those who reject Him.

But what about daily life, when we are walking through a seemingly endless trial that has become part of the normal routine? What about the days when our hearts are torn between enjoying present mercies from the Lord and the fearful thought that they could all be taken away in the blink of an eye? What about the days when we find ourselves wishing we could just "get it over with" and go through one big trial, rather than all the smaller—yet tiring, inconvenient, and demanding—hardships that come up? Do we respond by girding up the loins of our mind and saying, *Wait a minute, who is God in this? What does the gospel say about this?*

Does the gospel regularly interject our thoughts, emotions, and affections and fill us with renewed hope for all that is ours in Christ—both now and in eternity? Does the gospel meet us in our tears of stress, our tears of worry, our tears of pain, and even our tears of joy and quietly remind us, *There are better things to come?* Does the gospel make us laugh at the days to come? It should.

But if my mind is clouded by earthly cares; if my distracted thoughts are dragging me around in the dirt and hindering my mind's ability to get to work; if God's word is of little importance to me and has no effect on my response to another day of nerve pain or another problem with the minivan; if I am ignorant of eternal realities and yet fully attentive to earthly possibilities—*it won't.*

If we would be God-fearing, laughter-filled women whose responses to all the perplexities of life are molded by biblical answers about who God is and who we are, the gospel must matter to us. Its truths must become more to us than abstract, subjective ideas that can be explained but are not experienced—because apart from the gospel, there is nothing to laugh about. Apart from the gospel, we are among those who have "no hope and [are] without God in the world" (Eph. 2:12). Apart from the gospel, life will be a game of "suppose" and wishful thinking.

But we are not among those who have no hope because "according to his great mercy, he has caused us to be born again to a living hope through the resurrection of Jesus Christ from the dead" (1 Peter 1:3 ESV), and therefore we are no longer ignorant of God but are rather among those whose eyes and ears have been opened. God's word and the Spirit who speaks to us through that word enable us to be sober, God-conscious women who are daily responding to the good, bad, and potential circumstances of life with calm and correct thinking. And it is this calm and correct thinking that allows us to fix our gaze—tear-filled as it may be—on heaven and that glorious day when sorrow and sighing shall flee away (Isa. 51:11).

For the next three chapters, we are going to look at specific gospel truths about the Father, the Son Jesus Christ, and the Holy Spirit, and how a correct understanding of these truths helps us to be women who are laughing at the days to come. The purpose of these chapters is not to leave us with a bunch of abstract or redundant statements about the gospel. Rather, we want to look at truths that will actually change the way we think and thus the way we live; truths that we will call to mind when the powerful emotions of fear and worry are pulling us in the other direction; truths that help us respond to life with God-consciousness.

I am not going to simply tell you, "'For God so loved the world that He gave His only begotten Son, that whoever believes in Him should not perish but have everlasting life' (John 3:16), therefore, don't be discouraged, but laugh! You are on your way to heaven!" That is true for the Christian, but we need to go a little deeper than that. We need to ask, *What is the character of this God of the gospel and how does He relate to me in my suffering? What is His disposition toward me? What is true about God and His work in the gospel that should make me laugh, rejoice, and smile at the days to come?*

To be certain, this will not be an exhaustive examination of the work of the Trinity in salvation and suffering. But we do not need to be scholars before we can think soundly, and we do not need to be exhaustive before we can set our feet on a path to a more thorough understanding.

As God grants us discernment, may we be women who know more fully and think more clearly. For only then, with the loins of our minds girded, will we be able to hope more fearlessly.

HER COMFORT
God's Fatherly Sovereignty

And you have forgotten the exhortation which speaks to you
as to sons:
> "My son, do not despise the chastening of the LORD,
> Nor be discouraged when you are rebuked by Him;
> For whom the LORD loves He chastens,
> And scourges every son whom He receives."
>
> —Hebrews 12:5–6

That which should distinguish the suffering of believers from
unbelievers is the confidence that our suffering is under the
control of an all-powerful and all-loving God. Our suffering
has meaning and purpose in God's eternal plan, and He brings
or allows to come into our lives only that which is for His glory
and our good.

—Jerry Bridges, *Trusting God*

When I set out to write this chapter, our family was getting ready to
leave for a vacation to Lake Michigan. Just days before we left, there
was a tragic story in the news about a small tour boat in Branson,
Missouri, that got caught in a sudden thunderstorm and sank. Of
the thirty-one people on the boat, seventeen drowned. In one group
of relatives on board, all nine survived. They were the only family on
the boat in which no one was lost.

A separate group of extended family had a very different
experience—of the eleven on board, nine were lost. The woman

from that family who survived lost her husband and all three of her young children. The family had originally considered going to Florida but in the end decided on Branson because Florida was too far. They had intended to go on the 6 p.m. boat tour that evening but accidentally drove to the wrong location, which landed them on the 6:30 p.m. tour instead—the one that ended in a horrifying tragedy. As I bought groceries, did laundry, and packed suitcases, it was hard to get that story out of my mind. *They were just a family going on vacation like us.*

The day we left, my husband mentioned to me that it might be wise to buy our boys swim shirts that have floaties built in to them because Lake Michigan is known to have particularly dangerous undercurrents that result in many drownings each year. After quickly browsing the Internet to see how much the swim shirts might cost us, I did another search: "drownings each year in Lake Michigan." I read a small snippet of information, and two thoughts came to mind: (1) *We need to be very, very careful;* and (2) *What if something happens and someone from our family becomes the next statistic?*

With the boat accident story fresh on my mind and the Internet statistics staring me in the face, there was an obvious opportunity for me to start playing the game of "suppose": *Suppose one of the boys or their cousins is pulled out into a current and vacation takes a terrible turn? Suppose we get in a car accident on the way there and vacation never begins in the first place?*

As I said in the last chapter, when we find ourselves in a difficult circumstance (or playing the game of "suppose" and thinking about a potential one), we often think primarily about how that circumstance affects the way we feel—sorrow, loss, physical pain, anger, stress, and resentment. And the emotions and internal struggles that result from various trying circumstances, as well as the anxiety we experience when we simply imagine them happening, end up being a trial in themselves, intensifying the struggle as a whole. But the sober-minded way to think in any circumstance, as we saw, is with an ever-present God-consciousness, asking not, How does this make me feel? but, Who is God in this?

When it comes to trials and suffering, however, this is not always a comfortable question to ask. But ask we must:

- Is God a sovereign king? Does He ordain my trials and then sovereignly bring them about in His own power and providence?

- Is God an angry judge? Is He punishing me for a specific sin? Is my suffering simply my own fault, the consequences for my own mistakes?

- Is God a good, loving, and trustworthy Father? How do I joyfully and confidently serve Him when I am uncertain of what He has ordained for the days to come?

These are not easy questions. Whether our minds are filled with anxious thoughts as we fearfully look toward the future or we are already knee-deep in the trenches of sorrow wondering what more is to come, these questions prick and pierce our hearts, forcing us to stare Scripture in the face and think honestly about our relation to its Author.

But if we ignore these questions and make no effort to answer them, we will fall prey to the whims of emotion and the danger of subtly unsound thoughts about God, which will directly affect how we respond in difficult circumstances—as women whose lives are marked by fear, anxiety, and the game of "suppose," or women whose lives are marked by a valiant, eternity-minded rejoicing in which God is glorified and fear has no final word.

So who is this God who makes us to be women—tired, sorrowful, hurting women—who are yet laughing? His word, and the glorious gospel it proclaims, gives us every answer we need. Let's start by laying a foundation with the first question: Is God a sovereign king? Does He ordain my trials and then sovereignly bring them about in His own power and providence? A correct answer to this question lays a necessary foundation for the questions that follow it (see above) and will help us bridge the gap between God's sovereignty, our suffering, and the gospel.

Shamelessly Sovereign

I think it's safe to say that most, if not all, confessing Christians would agree with the statement, "God is powerful." Likewise, we are quick to throw out comforting statements such as "God is in control!" and "God answers prayer!" But when the suffering is real, when the pain is deep, when the anxiety is overwhelming, when the pleading goes unanswered, we need more than surface-level slogans. How powerful is God? How much control does He really have? Scripture in no way leaves these questions unanswered and is quite unapologetic in its assertion that God is entirely and eternally sovereign. And when I say *sovereign*, I am talking about more than God causing the winds and waves to cease or taking note of the sparrow that falls to the ground, though these are certainly included. I am talking about a sovereignty that ordains and controls every miscarriage, every job loss, every cancer diagnosis, every toddler tantrum, every house fire, every false accusation, and every soul that rejects Christ and is separated from God forever. That list may make you uncomfortable. If so, stay with me and ask God for the grace to let Scripture have the final word.

An exhaustive exploration and defense of God's sovereignty is, of course, beyond the purpose of this chapter and the scope of this book. But Scripture does not stutter on this matter. I believe that one of the biggest difficulties we face when hesitating to embrace it is simply a lack of willingness to acknowledge that because we are finite creatures and not the all-knowing Creator, there will be a limit to our understanding; there will be a degree of mystery. Mystery, however, will not be a hindrance for the humble, but unbelief toward the truths plainly revealed in God's word will certainly harm the proud.[1]

---

1. If the doctrine of God's sovereignty is new to you and you would like to explore it more deeply, I recommend the following excellent and reader-friendly resources for further study: A. W. Pink, *The Sovereignty of God* (Edinburgh: Banner of Truth, 1961); Joel R. Beeke, *Living for God's Glory: An Introduction to Calvinism* (Orlando, Fla.: Reformation Trust, 2008); R. C. Sproul, *Chosen by God* (Carol Stream, Ill.: Tyndale House, 1986); Loraine Boettner, *The Reformed Doctrine of Predestination* (Phillipsburg, N.J.: P&R, 1932).

Let's take a brief but compelling look at what the Bible tells us about God's sovereign control of the universe:

God is sovereign over the number of man's days:

> Now see that I, even I, am He,
> And there is no God besides Me;
> I kill and I make alive;
> I wound and I heal;
> Nor is there any who can deliver from My hand.
> (Deut. 32:39)

The plans and purpose of God cannot be thwarted by people:

> The LORD brings the counsel of the nations to nothing;
> He makes the plans of the peoples of no effect.
> The counsel of the LORD stands forever,
> The plans of His heart to all generations. (Ps. 33:10–11)

Remember the image we saw in Psalm 2 of God laughing (see chapter 2)? The kings and rulers of the earth gather together to set themselves against God and His Anointed, and God laughs at this. Because He sits enthroned in the heavens doing whatever He pleases (Ps. 115:3), He is not threatened or thrown off guard by the evil plans and purposes of people. Additionally,

- God is sovereign over the weather (Ps. 135:6–7).
- God is sovereign over the animals—from the largest whale to the smallest worm (Jonah 1:17; 4:7).
- God is sovereign over earthly turmoil (Isa. 45:7; Amos 3:6).
- God is sovereign over disability and disease (Ex. 4:11; Job 2:7–10).
- God is sovereign over people and all their actions (Prov. 20:24; 21:1).
- God is sovereign over people's salvation (Rom. 9:15–18).

Paul sums it up well when he says that God "works all [all!] things according to the counsel of His will" (Eph. 1:11). And while the above verses skim only the surface of what Scripture has to say about God's sovereignty, they stand alone as a powerful testimony, compelling us to echo the awe-filled doxology:

> Oh, the depth of the riches both of the wisdom and knowledge of God! How unsearchable are His judgments and His ways past finding out!
>
> "For who has known the mind of the LORD?
>   Or who has become His counselor?"
> "Or who has first given to Him
>   And it shall be repaid to him?"
>
> For of Him and through Him and to Him are all things, to whom be glory forever. Amen. (Rom. 11:33–36)

Two Clarifications

Theologian Loraine Boettner candidly describes God's sovereignty when he writes,

> By virtue of the fact that God has created every thing which exists, He is the absolute Owner and final Disposer of all that He has made. He exerts not merely a general influence, but actually rules in the world which He has created.... Amid all the apparent defeats and inconsistencies of life God actually moves on in undisturbed majesty. Even the sinful actions of men can occur only by His permission. And since he permits not unwillingly but willingly, all that comes to pass—including the actions and ultimate destiny of men—must be, in some sense, in accordance with what He has desired and purposed.[2]

These are bold words, but because they are simply an echo of what Scripture clearly teaches, we ought not to shrink back from them. We may, with humble conviction and holy confidence, believe these truths to be correct not because we want them to be but because God has proclaimed them in His own word with undeniable clarity.

---

2. Boettner, *Reformed Doctrine of Predestination*, 30.

Yet because these truths are weighty and frequently misunderstood, it is important to clarify what we don't mean when we proclaim that God is sovereign over all things, including our suffering. For that reason, I would like to make two clarifications that I hope will shed further light on the nature of God's governance over all things.

First, when we ascribe the suffering of people to God's sovereignty, we are not nullifying people's responsibility for sin or making God the author of sin. When we declare God's sovereignty over all things, we assert that while He does ordain sin to take place, He does not perform or commit sin in a sense that would make Him guilty of it. The author-story illustration is helpful here.[3] The author of a mystery novel will use certain characters, actions, and events to develop the desired plot and arrive at the final outcome she has planned. She may write a murder into her story to serve a specific purpose in her plot, but we would not say that the author herself is guilty of murder; rather, the character in the story is guilty and rightfully tried and sentenced.

In the same way, it is God's will for the sin of people and the general curse of sin on the world to be a part of His perfect story of redemption for humankind. God does not commit the sin, but He does decree and ordain it for a holy purpose that sometimes is beyond our understanding.

There are many helpful examples of this in Scripture, but we will look at just two. In the book of Genesis, Joseph's brothers act wickedly against him by selling him into slavery. Years later Joseph tells his brothers, "But as for you, you meant evil against me; but God meant it for good, in order to bring it about as it is this day, to save many people alive" (Gen. 50:20). Note that Joseph does not say God had nothing to do with his brothers' actions and simply used His power to "clean up" their sinful mess and use it for Joseph's good. Near the end of the story Joseph says, "So now it was not you who

---

3. John M. Frame, *The Doctrine of God* (Phillipsburg, N.J.: P&R, 2002), 156–58.

sent me here, but God" (Gen. 45:8). His brothers meant it for evil, and thus they committed sin against Joseph. But as God ordained and then governed that sin, He had a different meaning in mind— one that would do good to Joseph and the nation of Israel.

We see the second example in the crucifixion and death of Christ. In Acts, a group of believers prays, "For truly against Your holy Servant Jesus, whom You anointed, both Herod and Pontius Pilate, with the Gentiles and the people of Israel, were gathered together to do whatever Your hand and Your purpose determined before to be done" (4:27–28). It was God's sovereignly ordained plan and purpose that Christ would be crucified, but as the author of the story, He chose to bring about that plan by the sinful actions of Herod, Pilate, and many others.

Second, when we ascribe the suffering of people to God, we do not nullify the involvement of Satan. We mustn't forget that Satan "walks about like a roaring lion, seeking whom he may devour" (1 Peter 5:8) and that we are called to put on the armor of God so as to "stand against the wiles of the devil" (Eph. 6:11). Satan does have power and is ever seeking to use it to make us fall into sins and circumstances that would bring much suffering and sorrow on us.

But it is equally important to remember that the Bible shows us that Satan may not afflict people apart from God's sovereign consent. In the first two chapters of Job, Satan is granted permission twice to plunge Job into a great valley of suffering. The first time, Satan is allowed to touch Job's children and possessions, but not Job himself (Job 1:12). The second time, Satan is allowed to touch Job but not to the point of death (Job 2:6). Even the evil work of Satan is governed and granted by God. Rather than frustrating God's plan, Satan's work furthers it because it is already a part of the story God has written. In other words, Satan has a *role*, but he does not *rule*. Whether these truths are difficult or easy for us to accept, let us remember that any "God-consciousness" we have will not be a help to us if our thoughts about Him are not truly in alignment with His word.

There's More to Suffering than Sovereignty

During those first years of progressive hearing loss, I did not have a very solid theology of the relationship between suffering and God's sovereignty. For a long time, I saw God as a taker. He took my hearing, and with it some of my dreams for the future. (Remember the overseas ministry I was going to start before I remembered I wouldn't be able to hear?) I did end up going overseas to be a missionary for a short time, but when that did not go as planned, I decided that God took the "missionary dream" from me as well. I did not like the thought that God wanted to take things from me and wondered what He was going to take next.

Interestingly, I had part of my theology right at this point—God, in His sovereignty, actually *does* take away. The best example we have of this in Scripture is, again, in the story of Job. Right after Job learns that he has lost his servants, his possessions, and even all his children, he falls to the ground in humble worship and exclaims,

> Naked I came from my mother's womb,
> And naked shall I return there.
> The LORD gave, and the LORD has taken away;
> Blessed be the name of the LORD. (Job 1:21)

The next verse tells us that Job "did not sin nor charge God with wrong." God did no wrong in taking from Job, and it was not wrong for Job to attribute that taking to God because it was a correct declaration of God's sovereignty over his life.

God had sovereignly taken my hearing—of this much I was aware. But the fact of God's sovereignty over my hearing loss in and of itself was not much help. Thinking about God as simply a "taker" made it difficult for me to turn to Him for comfort. I wanted to see Him as a loving and compassionate God who desired to *give* and not just take, but as I bitterly clung to my own notions, I could not.

Let's be honest about something: when it comes to the pain or prospect of trials and suffering, the acknowledgment of God's sovereignty is not in itself sufficient to make us women who laugh at the days to come. God is sovereign, but what is it about God in His sovereignty that ought to comfort and strengthen my restless heart? Why should I not be fearful of His sovereignty if at any moment He could ordain death, disease, or disobedient kids? Why should I not be anxious about the things He might bring about in the future? This is where the gospel comes in.

The gospel was missing from my view of God, and therefore I had a wrong understanding of what kind of God was doing the taking. I thought of myself as a true Christian who had been saved by God's grace, but I didn't yet understand how the gospel ought to affect my thinking toward the trials of life—more particularly, how it ought to affect my thinking toward God's sovereignty over those trials. God was sovereign, but with what disposition was He working out that sovereignty in my life?

When we bring the gospel to this question, it radically transforms our understanding of suffering—the big trials, the small discomforts, the daily inconveniences, the heartbreaking losses, the confusing conflict, and everything in between.

Why does the gospel radically transform our understanding of suffering? *Because it radically changes our relationship with the all-powerful God of the universe.* Paul describes this changed relationship:

> But when the fullness of the time had come, God sent forth His Son, born of a woman, born under the law, to redeem those who were under the law, that we might receive the adoption as sons....
>
> Therefore you are no longer a slave but a son, and if a son, then an heir of God through Christ. (Gal. 4:4–5, 7)

The work of Christ made a way for children of wrath (Eph. 2:3) to become children of God. Therefore we are "no longer strangers and foreigners, but fellow citizens with the saints and members of the household of God" (Eph. 2:19). This entry into the household of God is a high privilege only for those who have put their trust in Christ for their salvation. Some people are often quick to tell anyone and everyone that they are children of God, but biblically speaking that is not the case. All people are created by God, but only those who are born again become children of God.

Why does this matter, and how does it affect my response to the trials and uncertainties of life? Simply put, if I am a child of God, then God is my Father. Because God is my Father, His sovereignty in my life is a *fatherly* sovereignty. And it is this fatherliness that makes a world of difference in an earthly life of pain and perplexity.

To believe that God governs all things, including any present and future suffering we experience, is certainly a step in the right direction. This is not an easy truth for us to climb on board with because it stretches our minds and challenges our natural, human-centered ways of thinking. But when we humbly embrace this truth and then take it a step further by uniting it with the reality of our adoption into the household of God, His sovereignty over life's suffering becomes a sweet refuge—not a power from which we run, but a promise in which we rest.

Perhaps this truth has something to do with why in his first epistle Peter does not apologize to his readers about their suffering or try to excuse God from the picture and blame it all on Satan. Satan did have a role in their suffering (1 Peter 5:8–9), but Peter has no problem assigning their suffering to God's will: "Therefore let those who suffer according to the will of God commit their souls to Him in doing good, as to a faithful Creator" (4:19; cf. 3:17). But Peter does not leave the gospel out of the picture because it is the very thing that will allow his readers to acknowledge God's hand in their suffering and yet at the same time rejoice and look to the future with hope. He reminds them that they are "elect according to the foreknowledge of God the Father" (1:2), with an unfading inheritance waiting for them in heaven (v. 4). God is not only their faithful Creator but also their loving Father, who is wielding His great power to ensure that His children arrive safely home to receive their inheritance (v. 5).

For Us, Not Against Us

When I saw God as a taker, I thought of Him as a God who had control, but not as a God who cared. Coldness and carelessness, however, are not the ways in which a good and perfect father deals with his children, and they are not ways God deals with His children. When we detach God's sovereignty from His fatherliness, it causes us to look on our suffering as something God is doing *to* us, and we are fearful because He may soon do something else and there is no getting away from it. But how does a good and perfect father (which God is) deal with his children? When He sovereignly takes away, is He doing something *to* His children or *for* His children? Is He acting with a desire to hurt or a desire to help?

In Romans 8 we find a precious promise that speaks of how God deals with His children:

> And we know that all things work together for good to those who love God, to those who are the called according to His purpose....
> If God is for us, who can be against us? (Rom. 8:28, 31)

As He sovereignly works *all* things according to the purpose of His will, He is making *all* things work together for good to whom? To those who are "called according to His purpose." This is an exclusive promise for the children of God. When God gives to His children, He does it for their good. When God takes from His children, He does it for their good. His sovereignty is never working *against* His children, but is always working *for* them. He is not a cold Father, but a concerned Father who is not harsh in His dealings, but holy.

Unfortunately, I did not understand this while I was losing my hearing, and the idea of God as a taker was not the only incorrect view I had of Him. I clearly remember a season when I could not shake the image of God shooting arrows at me—not to help me, but to hurt me. I did not have biblical grounds for this view, but because I lacked a sound God-consciousness, I indulged it rather than rejecting it.

Once again, my theology was half correct—we do find God shooting arrows in the Bible. But at whom does He shoot them? In Psalm 64, David prays that God would hide him

from the secret plots of the wicked . . .
        who aim bitter words like arrows,
    shooting from ambush at the blameless. (vv. 2–4 ESV)

The wicked are shooting at David, "but God shall shoot at them
[the wicked] with an arrow; suddenly they shall be wounded"
(v. 7). Again, in Psalm 21 David speaks of those who hate God and
plan evil against Him: "Therefore You will make them turn their
back; You will make ready Your arrows on Your string toward their
faces" (v. 12).

The arrows of God's judgment and wrath are reserved not for
His beloved children but for the wicked who reject Him. What, then,
should we make of David in Psalm 38 who, when he feels the great
weight of his own sin, prays,

    O LORD, do not rebuke me in Your wrath,
    Nor chasten me in Your hot displeasure!
    For Your arrows pierce me deeply,
    And Your hand presses me down. (vv. 1–2)

Charles Spurgeon remarks, "It seems strange that the Lord should
shoot at his own beloved ones, but in truth he shoots at their sins
rather than them, and those who feel his sin-killing shafts in this life,
shall not be slain with his hot thunderbolts in the next world."[4] The
physical, emotional, or spiritual suffering (i.e., "arrows") David was
experiencing may have been a rebuke for his sin, but that rebuke did
not flow from the wrath God reserves for the unrepentant. The sav-
ing work of Christ ushers us into the household of God and makes
us His children, and therefore we receive not the wrath of God, but
the loving rod of God.

Discipline versus Punishment

In Hebrews 12 we find a helpful and comforting explanation of
God's fatherliness, which proves to be of great assistance when we

---

4. Charles H. Spurgeon, *The Treasury of David* (Grand Rapids: Zondervan,
1966), 1:198.

are trying to understand how the gospel affects His sovereign dealings with us:

> And you have forgotten the exhortation which speaks to you
> as to sons:
>
>> "My son, do not despise the chastening of the LORD,
>> Nor be discouraged when you are rebuked by Him;
>> For whom the LORD loves He chastens,
>> And scourges every son whom He receives." (vv. 5–6)

The idea that God disciplines us is not always a pleasant
thought—especially when that discipline brings with it some form
of discomfort. We automatically associate it with the word *punishment*, envisioning it alongside harshness or a disappointed frown,
perhaps as we remember the imperfect ways of our parents or as we
wrestle with our own struggle to discipline our children with love
and patience.

But when it comes to God's fatherly sovereignty in our lives, it
is vital that we have a correct and gospel-saturated understanding
of His fatherly discipline toward us. If we are without this, we will
wrongly view our suffering as something God is doing *to* us rather
than *for* us. As Sara Wallace helpfully points out, there is a significant difference between punishment and discipline: "Discipline may
look and feel similar to punishment, but they are radically different.
Discipline has a completely different motive: love. Discipline doesn't
seek retribution. It genuinely seeks the best for the other person."[5]

Why is God seeking our best? Why does He not seek retribution toward us? Why is His motive love? The answer is, Christ has
already paid for our sin, and the judgment and wrath of God toward
that sin has been satisfied. Let us be certain of this: those who have
believed in Christ for their salvation and have God as their Father
do not and never will pay for their sins because Christ already has.
Therefore, if God ordains for us to walk through some painful loss,

---

5. Sara Wallace, *For the Love of Discipline: When the Gospel Meets Tantrums and
Time-Outs* (Phillipsburg, N.J.: P&R, 2018), 28.

debilitating disease, or stressful financial conflict, we must be quick to think biblically about the nature of God's sovereign activity in those things—that He is a good and wise Father who allows His children to suffer not because He desires their pain but because He desires their profit. Hebrews 12 goes on to say, "For [earthly fathers] indeed for a few days chastened us as seemed best to them, but He for our profit, that we may be partakers of His holiness" (v. 10).

The greatest profit our trials and suffering could bring us is the great happiness of holiness—holiness both on earth and in heaven, where it will one day be perfect. And this is what our Father is working toward at all times, whether He works through blessings or buffetings. He desires our highest good, and our highest good is God-glorifying, Christ-exalting, Spirit-enabled holiness. When God shoots His sin-killing arrows, we may indeed be pained by His discipline—"nevertheless, afterward it yields the peaceable fruit of righteousness to those who have been trained by it" (Heb. 12:11).

Did I Sin or Did I Not?

One reason we may have a hard time talking about God's discipline in the context of our suffering is because sometimes we cannot be sure of the exact reason for it. *Are these trials God's discipline for past sin? If so, which sin? What if He is rebuking me for a sin I am not aware of?* While it is always good to search our hearts and ask God to show us our sin so that we can confess and repent of it, it is possible to be so introspective that we grow weary, discouraged, and paranoid, constantly wondering if we are being chastised for sin. As we see in the story of Job, sometimes God's discipline is not a rebuke or chastisement for sin, but something He is simply allowing for our spiritual growth.

Bottom line: we do not always know the reason for our trials, and sometimes there will be mystery. And while it certainly is not wrong to ask *why* in our suffering, especially out of desire to deal with sin, the greater focus should be on the *who*. Instead of asking, Why am I suffering this particular trial? we can instead ask, Who is God in this particular trial? The trials of those who reject Christ and remain in darkness are glimpses of God's just and holy judgment on sin and a foretaste of the wrath to come. But the trials of those who have put their trust in Christ and call on God as Father are a sweet reminder that a sovereign and loving hand is at work—even when they have sinned—for their highest joy and greatest good.

Yes, our sin does have consequences. But when the sovereign King is our Father, those consequences are never mere consequences. They are providences—acts of love designed to carry out His plan and purpose for the people in whom He delights.[6] It is in this love-filled, fatherly sovereignty of God that the gospel compels us to hope (confidently expect) through all our days of earthly troubles. As we do so, we have the comfort of knowing that God does not despise us as we look to Him for love, but "the LORD takes pleasure…in those who hope in his steadfast love" (Ps. 147:11 ESV).

The family vacation I mentioned at the beginning of the chapter is over now. We all arrived home safely and thanked God for it. My husband's glasses broke the first day we were there, and the rental home's septic tank started overflowing the last day, but other than that, we had a pretty problem-free vacation. I do not know why God chose to bless my family with safety while we drove on the highway and swam in Lake Michigan. But this I do know: even if He had not, He still would have been the same father He was the day we left for the trip. The nature of His sovereignty toward me is secured by the precious blood of Christ, and in that truth my heart must rest and rejoice.

---

6. I am indebted to Pastor Dale Van Dyke for pointing this out in his sermon on Hebrews 12:3–11 entitled "Faith in the Pain," preached on July 1, 2018, at Harvest Orthodox Presbyterian Church in Wyoming, Michigan.

Seven

HER GUIDE
Christ's Perfect Example

For to this you were called, because Christ also suffered for us,
leaving us an example, that you should follow His steps:
"Who committed no sin,
Nor was deceit found in His mouth."

—1 Peter 2:21–22

Like many of the Puritans of his time, John Flavel was a man familiar with great suffering. His parents were imprisoned for holding
an illegal worship service and shortly after their release died from
the plague. His first wife died in childbirth, and he went on to lose
both his second and third wives. Only his fourth wife outlived him.
Furthermore, because he was a nonconformist minister, he often
faced the threat of persecution and was eventually expelled from the
Church of England.[1] Thankfully, Flavel did not let his suffering go
to waste and wrote extensively on the subject during his lifetime,
a labor that has greatly benefited those who have taken the time to
learn from him.

As I recently read about Flavel's profound views on suffering,
I was helped by a particular term he liked to use when referring to
the suffering of believers. Making a careful distinction between the
trials of the unbeliever and the believer, he referred to the Christian's

---

1. Brian Cosby, *Suffering and Sovereignty: John Flavel and the Puritans on Afflic-
tive Providence* (Grand Rapids: Reformation Heritage Books, 2012), 3–4.

suffering as "sanctified afflictions." Brian Cosby explains, "While affliction and suffering come upon the unbeliever as signs of God's judgment and wrath, they come upon the elect as loving discipline with a design to produce greater godliness. The only reason for the change in the goal of each particular suffering is whether it has been 'sanctified' through Christ's sacrifice of atonement."[2] Quoting Flavel, Cosby then adds, "It is only through 'the efficacy and virtue of Christ's blood' that 'sanctified afflictions…produce such blessed effects upon the soul.'"[3] In the last chapter, we saw that our adoption into God's family transforms our perspective of suffering because it compels us to see every trial, frustration, and discomfort as coming from the sovereign hand of a *Father* who is always tenderly and wisely working all things for the good of His children. Knowing and believing this helps us to be women who laugh at the days to come, whether our pain is present or prospective. We mustn't fail to recognize, however, that the only reason we have the comfort of the sovereign God being our Father is because of the precious reality of Christ—the One who came to earth as man and mediator, living and dying as our perfect representative before God.

It is extremely important to have a right view of the Father as we walk through the trials and perplexities of life, but a right view of the Father must go hand in hand with a right view of His Son—for it is only because of Christ's mediatorial work in the gospel that we are able to joyfully claim and know God as our loving Father. Apart from Christ, there is nothing for me to laugh about because the sovereign ruler of the universe is not working for my good. Apart from Christ, I have no fatherly smile on me, but rather a constant foretaste of God's wrath. He has not been satisfied with any perfect payment for my sin, and thus I am barred from the comfort, love, and protection of His presence. Apart from Christ, I have no grounds to rejoice in a coming day when my tears will be wiped away, my suffering finished, and my hope fulfilled. Therefore, it is necessary to turn our

---

2. Cosby, *Suffering and Sovereignty*, 60.
3. Cosby, *Suffering and Sovereignty*, 60.

thoughts to the work of Christ in the gospel, for here we find much reason to laugh.

Many of us are able to describe the work of Christ to some extent. We could talk about the miracles He performed and some of the things He taught. We could explain in simple terms what happened to Him in His last hours and what people celebrate on Easter. But when it comes to walking through all the various afflictions life brings us, both small and great, who exactly is Christ to us, and how do we relate to Him? What is it about Christ that would enable me to laugh when I think about the possibility that in three years my nerve pain may be significantly worse? And what about the days when I find myself on the verge of tears because my tinnitus is screaming, my boys are disobeying, and my laundry piles are multiplying? God's fatherly sovereignty will no doubt be greatly comforting, but what knowledge and thoughts of Christ will bring respite to my downcast soul? The aim of this chapter and the next is to answer such questions and, in doing so, compel us toward a knowledge and cherishing of Christ that constantly affects the way we respond to all of life.

Looking unto Jesus

When it comes to wading through the many perplexities of life, most people would agree that men tend to approach situations with more simplicity than women. Let me give you an example from my dear husband. Sometimes I come to him with some kind of struggle; this or that is happening, my emotions are rampant, and everything is mingled with my own sin—sinful responses, sinful reliance on my feelings, sinful lack of Scripture-saturated thoughts. I'm discouraged or weary, and I want my husband to tell me something that will fix things, perhaps something I can go and *do*. And yet multiple times I have received this very simple response: "You need to look to Christ."

Sigh. There's that "Look to Christ" answer again. But isn't that precisely what Scripture tells me to do? The author of Hebrews exhorts, "Let us lay aside every weight, and the sin which so easily ensnares us, and let us run with endurance the race that is set before us, looking unto Jesus, the author and finisher of our faith" (12:1–2). In light of these verses, J. C. Ryle writes,

> The Christianity which the world requires…is a useful every-day religion. It is a healthy, strong, manly plant, which can live in every position, and flourish in every atmosphere, except that of sin. It is a religion which a man can carry with him wherever he goes, and never need leave behind him. In the army or in the navy, at the public school or at college, in the hospital-room or at the bar, on the farm or in the shop—true heaven-born Christianity will live and not die. It will wear, and stand, and prosper in any climate—in winter and in summer, in heat and in cold. Such a religion meets the needs of mankind. But where is such true Christianity to be found? What are its special ingredients? What is the nature of it? What are its peculiar characteristics?[4]

And what was his answer to his concluding questions? Ryle believed the answer to his questions was a life that is always, ever looking unto Jesus. Maybe my husband has been giving me the best answer all along.

Looking unto Jesus sounds good and right, but what is it about this simple solution that makes us raise our eyebrows in confusion? Why does it not resonate with us? Maybe we're not really sure what exactly we're supposed to look at, or such a solution seems too intangible and simplistic to be of any real help. Where should we start?

A Provision and a Pattern

Perhaps the best way to start is not by asking *how* to look but *why*. The writer of Hebrews does not leave us without an explanation as to why exactly we ought to be "looking unto Jesus" for endurance as we run our daily, heavenward race: "And let us run with endurance the race that is set before us, looking unto Jesus, *the author and finisher of our faith, who for the joy that was set before Him endured the cross,*

---

4. Ryle, "Looking unto Jesus!"

despising the shame, and has sat down at the right hand of the throne of God" (12:1–2, emphasis added).

When we are trying to run with endurance in a world that constantly burdens us with its fallen state, why must we look unto Jesus? The reason given is twofold: Jesus has shown us the perfect *pattern*, and He has made the perfect *provision* (as the "author and finisher of our faith")—and both of these are means toward a life of laughter. We will look at Christ's *pattern* in this chapter and His *provision* in the next chapter.

Christ, Our Supreme Example

As a mom, I am often grieved by my failure to set a godly example for my boys. I want to show them a right use of technology, and then catch myself glued to my phone. I want to show them the fruit of self-control, and then lose my patience and speak in an angry tone. I am so thankful that ultimately their salvation is not dependent on their mother's example.

When it comes to Jesus, however, it is a different story. The example He set for us during His earthly life was daily, entirely without sin. Ryle's words again paint a compelling picture:

> Let us Christians trace all the footsteps of our Master's career from the carpenter's workshop at Nazareth to the cross of Calvary.... He is always the same,—always holy, harmless, undefiled; always perfect in word and deed. Mark what a wonderful combination of seemingly opposite qualifications is to be seen in His character. Bold and outspoken in opposing hypocrisy and self-righteousness, tender and compassionate in receiving the chief of sinners; profoundly wise in arguing before the Sanhedrin; simple, so that a child might understand Him, in teaching the poor; patient towards His weak disciples; unruffled in temper by the keenest provocation; considerate for all around Him; sympathizing, self-denying, prayerful, overflowing with love and compassion, utterly unselfish, always about His Father's business, ever going about doing good, continually ministering to others, and never expecting others to

minister to Him,—what person born of woman ever walked on earth like Jesus of Nazareth?[5]

If we were given a snapshot of every moment of Jesus's life, all we would see is absolute holiness, utmost purity, and flawless love. When Jesus washed His disciples' feet, He told them that He had given them an example, that they should do as He had done (John 13:15). He was able to say that with all sincerity because He had not failed once to show them a perfect example of righteousness. And Scripture indeed tells us that Christ's life is the pattern our lives ought to emulate. We are to "walk just as He walked" (1 John 2:6). Paul writes to the Corinthians, "Imitate me, just as I also imitate Christ" (1 Cor. 11:1; cf. Eph. 5:1). Jesus is our supreme example of a holy and God-glorifying life, walked out perfectly in a world of sin and darkness.

Christ, the Perfect Sufferer

While Scripture gives us insight as to how we can imitate Christ in many areas of life, let's zoom in and think specifically about Christ's example in His suffering. We usually think primarily of the cross when we think about the afflictions of Jesus. While the cross was indeed the climax of His suffering, we mustn't have the idea that it was His only hour of trial. Among other things, some of which are likely not recorded in Scripture, here are a few of the difficulties Jesus went through during His earthly life:

- He was greatly misunderstood and rejected by His own family, as well as the people of His hometown (Matt. 13:57; Mark 3:21; John 7:1–5).

- He went through an intense time of being tempted by the devil (Matt. 4:1–11).

- He grieved the loss of loved ones (Matt. 14:1–13; John 11:35–36).

---

5. Ryle, "Looking unto Jesus!"

- He daily dealt with disciples who were slow of understanding (Mark 8:31–33; 9:33–37).

Jesus did not live a happy-go-lucky and trouble-free life. He was "a Man of sorrows and acquainted with grief" (Isa. 53:3). But the suffering would get worse—and Jesus knew it.

Sometimes when we look to the future we are filled with anxiety because of how uncertain we are about what is to come. *What difficulties are waiting for me just around the corner? Is it okay to laugh?* we wonder. Other times we are filled with anxiety because we are painfully aware that some form of present suffering only brings with it the likelihood of greater suffering down the road. In Jesus's case, He knew full well that the greatest suffering was yet to come. The agony of the impending cross was no surprise to Him. The Old Testament prophecies, which He was familiar with, made plain what was coming. If anyone ever had a good reason to look toward the days to come and sweat drops of blood, it was Jesus. As Jesus agonized on the ground in the garden of Gethsemane, He knew that soon He would be deserted by His closest friends, bloodied by the Roman scourge, and hung naked on a cross with nine-inch nails. But even this was not the worst of His suffering, and Jesus knew it.

The physical pain Jesus bore was excruciating, but it did not compare to the pain He experienced when the Father turned His face away and allowed His Son to be plunged into darkness. The weight of sin and the horror of God's holy wrath against it brought suffering unlike any person ever has or will experience. Robert Murray M'Cheyne described it like this: "He was without any comforts of God—no feeling that God loved him—no feeling that God pitied him—no feeling that God supported him. God was his sun before—now that sun became all darkness…. He was without God—he was as if he had no God. All that God had been to him before was taken from him now. He was godless—deprived of his God."[6]

---

6. Robert Murray M'Cheyne, *Sermons of the Rev. Robert Murray M'Cheyne* (Edinburgh: Banner of Truth, 1961), 47–49.

When I look to Christ, I look to a man—a real man—whose earthly days did not promise coming relief, but approaching pain; not increasing comfort, but certain distress. And He walked it perfectly, setting before us a pattern that comes to us in our grief, our confusion, our sin, and our pain and urges us to go and do likewise.

So much could be said about the suffering of Christ, but for our purposes, we will look at three particular aspects of Christ's sinless suffering, all of which serve as a profound exhortation as we think about and respond to our own unique trials. In our "looking unto Jesus," we ought to look at His *confident obedience,* His *humble others-centeredness,* and His *hopeful outlook* in the midst of immense afflictions.

His Confident Obedience

Jesus said, "For I have come down from heaven, not to do My own will, but the will of Him who sent Me" (John 6:38). This sums up one of the most prominent (if not the most prominent) themes of Jesus's life. He did not come to earth with His own agenda, but with the sole intention to carry out the work His Father had given Him to do. Jesus said, "My food is to do the will of Him who sent Me, and to finish His work" (John 4:34).

Notice the specific wording Jesus uses in the Gospels when He describes the One who sent Him. Over and over again, particularly in the gospel of John, Jesus speaks of being sent by and doing the will of the Father. For example, He says, "The Son can do nothing of Himself, but what He sees the Father do; for whatever He does, the Son does also in like manner" (John 5:19). Again He proclaims, "For I have not spoken on My own authority; but the Father who sent Me gave Me a command, what I should say and what I should speak" (John 12:49).

Whose will did Christ come to accomplish? Was it the will of a cruel master? No, Christ came to accomplish the will of the Father—*His* Father. As Christ underwent His afflictions, He did so with the confident assurance that He was living a life of obedience to a tender Father whose heart swelled with love and concern for the well-being of His Son. Was His Father the reigning King? Yes. Was He the omnipotent Ruler of the universe? Yes. But near and dear to the heart of Christ was the fact that this King was His *Father*, and thus He walked in constant assurance of His Father's love.

Christ's example of a will constantly submitted to and in unity with the will of God in heaven is indeed a sight to behold. His humble, willing obedience "to the point of death, even the death of the cross" (Phil. 2:8) is the pattern of all patterns. But what makes Christ's example here even more stunning is His unchanging conviction that the suffering He submits to is being governed by the One who called Him "beloved Son" (Matt. 17:5; Luke 3:22). There is an intimate and indestructible bond of love between the Son and the Father, and thus the Son does not shrink back when He receives the command to die from His Father (John 10:18).

In the last days and hours of His life, Jesus never lost sight of this paternal relationship, and it no doubt brought Him immense comfort as He anticipated the excruciating pain He would soon experience. In John 17, He begins His High Priestly Prayer with the words, "Father, the hour has come" (v. 1). Christ had been faithful to accomplish the work His Father gave Him to do (v. 4), but now the hour had come for this final and most agonizing work. Who is the God in heaven to the suffering Son now? He is Father.

Later, as Jesus knelt in the garden of Gethsemane, sweating drops of blood as the assignment of death and divine wrath loomed over Him, the words that came from His mouth are once again telling: "O My Father, if it is possible, let this cup pass from Me; nevertheless, not as I will, but as You will" (Matt. 26:39). And finally, as Jesus hung bloody and naked on a cross and was just about to breathe His last breath, He cried out in astonishing confidence and childlike trust: "Father, 'into Your hands I commit My spirit'" (Luke 23:46). Mark Jones sums it up well: "Was there a safer place for Christ to commend himself than into the Father's hands? Just as we cannot be snatched out of Christ's hands, neither could he be snatched out of the Father's hands. The words of Christ speak volumes about the type of God he was entrusting himself to: a loving Father."[7]

His Humble Others-Centeredness

With brevity and precision, Mark speaks plainly about the kind of life Jesus lived on earth: "For even the Son of Man did not come to be served, but to serve, and to give His life a ransom for many" (Mark 10:45). That Jesus lived a life of suffering is certainly a comfort, but the way He walked it out is nothing short of convicting. The Gospels paint a unified picture of a man whose life was beautifully others-centered.

As I previously noted, not only was Jesus's suffering present but it was also prospective. Even as He suffered loss and ridicule, He knew there was much more to come. If Jesus had come to be served, those three years of ministry captured in the Gospels would have looked entirely different. If in light of His present hardship and approaching death Jesus had decided to throw all His energy into self-care, self-pity, and self-service, His example would be quite easy for our self-loving, sin-infested hearts to follow. Who would have blamed Jesus for withdrawing from people as much as possible, especially needy lepers and immature disciples? Who would have blamed Him for saying no to ministry and preaching opportunities so He could spend more time journaling about His burdens or reading books on suffering? After all, people often make life difficult and complicated. When it feels like the weight of the world is bearing down on us, isn't it preferable to simply be left alone in peace and quiet?

I know the feeling. If there is one way that Jesus's example in suffering challenges me most, this is it. My hearing loss has profoundly impacted my ability to freely communicate with others and thrive socially. Social situations in general simply intimidate, frustrate, and tire me. Different occasions bring different thoughts to mind:

What if I won't understand her accent?

---

7. Mark Jones, *Knowing Christ* (Edinburgh: Banner of Truth, 2015), 150.

That group doesn't really understand how to include me in the conversation.

I know it takes effort to communicate with me, and I don't want to be a burden.

I don't feel like giving the energy to talk to anyone right now, so I'll just sit alone.

Thoughts like these often make me want to avoid people. And when I say, "avoid people," what I really mean is, *these thoughts make me turn inward and focus on myself and my circumstances.* They make me focus on *my* needs, *my* unique situation, *my* dignity, *my* feelings.

Yes, it is true that my situation makes it hard to communicate. Yes, it is true that people don't understand exactly what it's like to be deaf. And the same could be said about anyone's unique and difficult circumstance: *My situation makes it hard to* (insert any action that involves loving or serving others). *People don't understand what it's like to* (parent three kids under three, live with chronic pain, work through a husband's abuse, raise a child with special needs, and so on).

This inward-focused way of thinking and living is a temptation to us all at one time or another. Instead of living a life of laughter in which we entrust our days to God and freely give our time, love, and energy to others, our sorrows are further weighed down by self-pity.

The life of Jesus shows us another way. In countless moments when He could have easily been thinking about His own needs and comfort, He turned His attention to others to meet both physical and spiritual needs. One of my favorite examples of this is in Matthew 14. Jesus has just gotten word about the death of John the Baptist, who was cruelly beheaded. This is a profound loss for Jesus, and no doubt His pain is great. In His grief, He gets into a boat and goes to a desolate place. Understandably, Jesus feels the need for time alone—to think, to mourn, to pray—perhaps even to ponder the reality of His own approaching death. But His time alone is short-lived because the crowds decide to follow Him. And when Jesus comes up to the shore and sees this crowd, Matthew tells us that He has compassion on them and heals the sick among them. When evening comes and everyone is hungry, not even then does Jesus try to excuse Himself by sending the crowd away. Instead, He multiplies bread and fish so that everyone can go home with stomachs full and souls touched.

In humility, Christ always counted others as more significant than Himself. Even as He suffered, He did not look only to His own interests but also to the interests of others (Phil. 2:3–4). Rather than avoid the situations that would demand His time, energy, and compassion, He walked right into them. His life of suffering was not an excuse to seek ease and isolation. His own needs and concerns did not blind His eyes from the needs and concerns of others. And this was the way He lived until the moment He died. In fact, He exhibited this others-centeredness in the hours leading up to His death.

As He awaited arrest, Jesus the Shepherd thought about His sheep and prayed that His Father would protect, keep, and unify them (John 17). As the nails were driven into His hands, Jesus the Great Physician considered the depraved state of His crucifiers and prayed that His Father would forgive them (Luke 23:34). As He hung from the cross, bloody and weak, Jesus the carpenter's son thought about His widowed mother and provided for her needs (John 19:26–27). As He prepared to breathe His last, Jesus the Savior of sinners had compassion for the criminal beside Him and opened His mouth with a promise of salvation (Luke 23:42–43). And as His heart stopped beating and the curtain tore in two, His others-centeredness reached a climax as He freely gave His life as a ransom for many.

His Hopeful Outlook

As Jesus was about to die, He cried out, "My God, My God, why have You forsaken Me?" (Matt. 27:46). We cannot deny that at this moment there was a real sense in which the Father had forsaken His Son. As M'Cheyne described it above, Jesus was here without the sense that His Father loved Him and cared for Him. The cup of His Father's wrath was not abstract or theoretical—it was real, and Jesus drank it fully. And thus He wholeheartedly echoed the cry of David in Psalm 22.

But do these words contain anything more than utter despair? Are these hopeless words, or are they hopeful words? Is Jesus merely looking to the impending hours of agony and the bitter cup He must drink? Where is the final gaze of the dying Savior? Hebrews 12:2 tells us that Jesus endured the cross "for the joy that was set before Him." Had Jesus merely been looking to the moments at hand, there would be no motivation to endure the pain of the cross. But as Jesus prepared to drink the cup of God's wrath down to the dregs, He knew full well that His endurance would end in exaltation. He would die a painful death, but He would not lie forsaken in the grave forever. He knew that the psalmist's prayer of despair (Ps. 22:1–21) gives way to shouts of praise and awe-filled worship among the nations (vv. 22–31).

When Jesus cried out to the Father, "Why have You forsaken Me?" He already knew the answer: "As Moses lifted up the serpent in the wilderness, even so must the Son of Man be lifted up, that whoever believes in Him should not perish but have eternal life" (John 3:14–15). The Son of Man had to be lifted up on the cross to die, lifted up from the grave alive, and lifted up into the heavenly places to sit enthroned in glory. This was the plan of redemption that He and His Father had agreed on. Christ was confident that as He died according to His Father's will, so the Father would grant His desire for the elect, His bride, to be with Him forever in glory.

It's interesting to note that the psalmist makes a bold declaration about both the past and the present:

> But You are holy,
> Enthroned in the praises of Israel.
> Our fathers trusted in You;
> They trusted, and You delivered them. (Ps. 22:3–4)

What did God do in the past? He delivered His people. Who is God right now, in the present? He is holy. This is sober-minded suffering at its best! And it gives way to the hope-filled declaration that though the Father has turned His face away for a moment, He

> has not despised nor abhorred the affliction of the afflicted;
> Nor has He hidden His face from Him;
> But when He cried to Him, He heard. (v. 24)

The Father will hear the cries of His Son and receive His perfect payment for the sins of His people, raising Him from the dead and seating Him at His right hand in the heavenly places (Eph. 1:20).

Jesus did not crumble on the cross. He looked ahead to the unclouded day of eternity and was our ultimate example of one who laughs at the days to come. The mark of one who laughs at the days to come is not a denial of pain and sorrow. Jesus was not ashamed to acknowledge that He had been forsaken. But the distinguishing mark of laughter at the days to come is an unwavering confidence that God will carry out His promises and finish what He began. Though the sorrow may last for the night, there is a coming joy that will not be taken away. This was the joy set before Jesus in His suffering, and He hoped for it to the very end.

Looking and Laughing

Jesus suffered profusely, but through it all He lived a life of obedience with an eye to the Father's love, selflessness with an eye to the needs of others, and hope with an eye to eternity. How does the perfect example of Jesus help us to laugh at the days to come? It confronts us in our selfishness, unbelief, and shortsightedness and says, "That is not the way—look instead at Jesus!"

When we want to doubt the Father's love and cherish thoughts that are not in alignment with His word; when our obedience is hesitant because we imagine ourselves submitting to a cold master, Jesus says, "No, My beloved, the Father Himself loves you—even as He loved Me" (see John 16:27; 17:23). "Every cross He sovereignly allows and every act of obedience He justly commands come from the heart of a Father who desires only good toward His children. I believed this to the grave, and I sit now at His right hand."

When we are tempted to let the burdens of life give way to self-pity and an inward gaze, Jesus says, "No, My beloved, that will not bring you happiness and relief! Look to Me, the Suffering Servant, and believe that great joy and satisfaction await the one who does not let her appointed cross keep her from her appointed mission."

When we want to cry at the days to come (or tomorrow, for that matter), Jesus says, "Look there, My beloved! Though the burdens of this earthly life are real, and though they are further weighed down by the reality of indwelling sin—you will not finally die, but live. I am coming to make all things new, and to this promise you must cling. The joy that was set before Me is now mine; endure, that it may one day be yours too."

We have not been left in the dark. The example of Christ is a guiding light that leads us on the path of suffering—suffering that results in both the creature's joy and the Creator's glory. May we rejoice in each daily opportunity to fix our eyes on His sinless life and holy laughter, wherein we find fresh encouragement to follow in His footsteps.

Eight

HER GUARANTEE
The Spirit's Enduring Preservation

For you died, and your life is hidden with Christ in God. When Christ who is our life appears, then you also will appear with Him in glory.
—Colossians 3:3–4

Why does the believer entertain the thought of God's determinate counsel with such joy? Why can he have patience in the perplexities and adversities of the present? Why can he have confident assurance with reference to the future and rejoice in hope of the glory of God? It is because he cannot think of past, present, or future apart from union with Christ.
—John Murray, *Redemption Accomplished and Applied*

When I was in sixth grade, there was a girl in my class I wanted to be like. We were good friends, but I always felt somewhat inferior to her. Heather had perfectly styled hair, and mine was a mass of frizzy curls. She was a great basketball player; I had tried the game in fifth grade, and let's just say it wasn't my sport. She also wore clothes from one of the most popular (and expensive) stores at the time. I did my best to dress stylishly but did not own a single item from that store. One time Heather let me borrow a shirt, but in the end I had to give it back and resort to the clothes in my own closet. When it came down to it, I simply didn't have the resources (i.e., the right hair, clothing, and skills) to be like her, and thus she remained a standard impossible for me to imitate.

Similarly, a beautiful cookbook photo of a three-layer carrot cake covered with cream cheese frosting is something I can try to replicate in my own kitchen. But if I don't have any carrots on hand, own no cake pans, and my oven is broken, the end product will hardly be a replica of the photo. A quick Google search may provide a few good hacks to help the process along, but the final appearance and taste would be far from the real thing. Without the right resources, there can be no replication—and this is why we once again need the gospel.

As discussed in the last chapter, Christ has left us with a stunning pattern for a life that suffers well and laughs at the days to come. But though His example encourages and motivates us, we must acknowledge that it also leaves us with a question: How can we ever attain to such a valiant pattern when even the smallest discomforts of life so often cause us to crumble? Is there more to the solution of looking unto Jesus than carefully observing His life and aiming to imitate Him?

The answer is yes. The gospel gives us not only a perfect pattern but also a perfect *provision*. It does not leave us merely inspired, but enabled. Because while we are called to follow in Christ's footsteps and walk as He walked, it does not take more than ten minutes for us to prove that, left to our own supply, *we don't have the resources needed for the replication*. If all we are doing in our looking unto Jesus is examining His sinless life and making our best effort to copy His words, actions, emotions, and responses, we will be left with nothing but frustration and failure.

Because of remaining sin, even the most zealous believer cannot suffer perfectly, as Jesus did. Therefore, though I may be motivated by His example, laughing at the days to come is quite difficult. I face not only the prospect of suffering but also the prospect of my sin that will mingle with that suffering.

We can try with all our might to be women who quietly endure pain and joyfully walk ahead toward an uncertain future, but our laughter will soon be turned to tears when we realize we don't even have what it takes to respond to the next hour, much less the next day, without sin. The pattern is good and needed, and it is right for us to look intently at it—but we need provision for the pattern. And that is exactly what we get in the gospel.

Having already looked at the Father and the Son, our aim in this chapter will be to think specifically about the person of the Holy Spirit. What exactly is provided for us in the gospel, and what does the Holy Spirit have to do with that provision? How does the ongoing work of the Holy Spirit compel us to be women who laugh at the days to come? If these are questions we seldom grapple with, we will miss out on truths that are meant to bring us much joy and encouragement.

Gospel Provision
So what is the provision? To put it precisely, the provision for the pattern is a Person. There are a lot of words we could use when we speak of what is provided for us in the gospel—justification, sanctification, adoption, and eternal life, among others. But what underlies all these is the plain and simple provision of a Person—Christ. And this is not simply a person we are looking at from a distance, like some dear, faraway friend whose occasional letters and phone calls bring us a measure of comfort and joy. Rather, we are given the profound gift of an intimate union with Christ—and the reality of this union is every ounce of provision we need for a Christianity that will "flourish in every atmosphere," as J. C. Ryle said. Let us not make the mistake of supposing that looking unto Jesus is straining our eyes to catch a glimpse of Him off in the distance, hoping to catch a sight of His smile or the faint sound of His voice encouraging us to press on and do the best we can. In our looking unto Jesus, we are fixing our gaze on a reality—a Person—to whom we are intimately bonded.

The Holy Spirit's Role
But isn't this chapter supposed to be about the Holy Spirit? Here I must clarify that it is the Holy Spirit, the Spirit of Christ, who actually executes and sustains our union with Christ. When we consider

the union between a husband and wife, we presuppose that we are thinking about two people who are alive at the same time and, apart from special exceptions, living in the same house and sleeping in the same bed. Though there are many ways a marriage union parallels our union with Christ, we need to recognize that the essence of our relationship with Christ differs from earthly marriage in certain ways. Obviously, the person of Christ is no longer living on earth in flesh and blood. Rather, He is seated at God's "right hand in the heavenly places," reigning "above all principality and power and might and dominion" (Eph. 1:20–21). He is there, but we are here. How, then, are we united?

Paul sheds light on the answer in his first letter to the Corinthians:

He who is joined to the Lord is one spirit with Him....

Or do you not know that your body is the temple of the Holy Spirit who is in you, whom you have from God, and you are not your own? (1 Cor. 6:17, 19)

Commenting on this passage, Sinclair Ferguson writes, "The Spirit who made Christ's body a temple dwells within us to fulfil the same function. Christ and we are possessed of one and the same Holy Spirit. He is the bond of an unbreakable union."[1] We cannot think about the power of the Holy Spirit working in and through us without also thinking about Christ. As new creations who are no longer united to Adam but are now united to Christ, we are indwelt by the same Spirit of holiness and power that dwells in His glorified humanity.

This is precisely what Jesus promised His disciples on the eve of His death: "I will not leave you orphans; I will come to you" (John 14:18). Jesus is promising His presence to be with the disciples, yet the context of the passage shows us that He is clearly referring to the Holy Spirit. "Christ sent the Spirit," explains Marcus Peter Johnson, "not so that we might have a roughly suitable replacement in his absence, but that we might enjoy the *actual presence of Christ*

---

1. Sinclair Ferguson, *The Holy Spirit* (Downers Grove, Ill.: InterVarsity Press, 1996), 107.

(through the Spirit). The Spirit is the personal manner or mode of Christ's dwelling in us."[2]

A Life-Transforming Union

When I think about marriage and, more specifically, my own marriage, there are several different benefits I could mention, all of which naturally go along with daily married life: help with the kids, financial support, free snow shoveling, dinner dates, verbal affirmation, and many more. But if while I was talking about my marriage I never once mentioned my husband's name, wouldn't that be strange? Marriage comes with a myriad of both benefits and obligations, all of which are good and right. And yet I did not enter into a covenant with a list of benefits; I entered into a covenant with a person. I did not become one flesh with the idea of marriage; I became one flesh with the person I married. So it is with our union with Christ. We know this because Paul parallels the marriage bond with Christ and His bride: "For we are members of His body, of His flesh and of His bones. 'For this reason a man shall leave his father and mother and be joined to his wife, and the two shall become one flesh.' This is a great mystery, but I speak concerning Christ and the church" (Eph. 5:30–32).

The Christian life is not an impersonal business transaction; it is not a onetime handout of spiritual blessings that provides us with the potential to become like Christ. His redemptive work does indeed supply us with the amazing benefits of justification, adoption, sanctification, and glorification, but the Spirit applies these to us *only as we are united to Christ*. We cannot think about the Holy Spirit working powerfully in and through us without also thinking about being in Christ. There is no other way to be made holy (and thus happy) than to be united to the perfectly Holy One. And that is exactly what God does for His beloved elect. He joins them to His Son in such a way that enables them to be vitally nourished, continuously transformed,

---

2. Marcus Peter Johnson, *One with Christ: An Evangelical Theology of Salvation* (Wheaton, Ill.: Crossway, 2013), 44, emphasis original.

and daily comforted by that union—or more precisely, by that Person to whom they are united.

Apart from being one with Christ, the Christian life becomes a stale and impersonal venture in which the hoped-for result is far too dependent on our own imagined ability to follow the instruction manual, stay calm in the process, and come out on the other side in one piece.

A couple years ago, my son got a battery-operated wooden 3-D puzzle for Christmas. The intended end result was a tyrannosaurus rex that actually moved and made noise—a pretty cool toy for a four-year-old boy. One afternoon, he and I decided to get out the puzzle and start the daunting assembly process. Unfortunately, our ambitions were short-lived. The instructions were less than crystal clear, and the pieces were not holding together well. As I tried to secure one of the small wooden pieces, it snapped in half and my frustrations mounted. I tried in vain to tape it together and soon wanted nothing more to do with this useless puzzle. We were unable to return it to the store, so it sat on a shelf for many months. Needless to say, my son never got his tyrannosaurus rex. Perhaps it was a "mom fail" and I should have taken the time to try again, but I'm pretty sure keeping the box closed and on the shelf saved us (both) from many a tear.

Imagine if the designer of the puzzle had actually showed up at our house to patiently guide us through the process of putting it together. What if when my hands fumbled and I snapped a piece in two he responded with a cheerful "No problem!" and quickly handed me a spare piece? What if he told us he would stay that afternoon until the entire puzzle was put together correctly? Obviously, it would have been an entirely different experience.

Without trying to stretch the analogy too far, it helps to think of the Christian's union with Christ in these terms. We do not just have a set of puzzle pieces, a somewhat clear instruction manual, and a picture of what the end result should look like. God does not hand His children a fantastic gift and say, "Enjoy this, and come show Me when you are finished!" He unites them to the "puzzle designer," if you will. And because of that, we do not look at the instructions with wide eyes and silent intimidation; we do not get halfway through and say, "There's no way I'm going to be able to finish this."

Unlike our efforts with the puzzle, however, we actually possess no ability at all to imitate the holy, laughter-filled life of Christ. Had we been determined enough, my son and I could have finished the puzzle by ourselves. Perhaps we would have needed only a few helps here and there from the puzzle designer. Maybe we would have even sent him home once we were close to the end product, confident we could finish on our own. In the Christian life, however, we are utterly without the ability to start, continue, or finish on our own. We are in need of much more than someone cheering us on from the sidelines and offering help when we get confused. We need the Spirit of Christ—the Holy Spirit—living in us and empowering us to imitate Christ.

Factored into Life

Explaining the Christian's relation to Christ, Michael Barrett writes, "As we live in this world, we are diligently and continually to bring heaven to bear on the issues of life. That we are united to Christ is for us a fact of life that we must factor into life."[3] Facts are good and helpful, but not all facts play an equally important role in life. It may be true that the population of China is over one billion people, but this is not a fact that affects my thinking and doing on a daily basis. The fact that I am a wife and mother, however, is certainly something that I must "factor into life" every day. The way I spend my time, the food I buy, the commitments I make, and many other decisions are all affected by the fact that I am a wife to Nick and a mama to two boys, ages four and six—whether they are awake and visible or asleep and out of my sight.

The believer's intimate union with Christ is not a magical doctrine that causes sin, sorrow, and sighing to disappear from life;

3. Michael P. V. Barrett, *Complete in Him: A Guide to Understanding and Enjoying the Gospel* (Grand Rapids: Reformation Heritage Books, 2017), 100.

knowledge of it will not typically change unfortunate circumstances. Nevertheless, it is an important truth that when factored into life will greatly affect the way I think about and respond to those circumstances. Because I am united to Christ, all my looking unto Jesus brings to mind not only what is true about Him but also what is true about me as I am united to Him.

I can know, believe, and perhaps even appreciate the fact that I am united to Christ by His Spirit; but it is another thing for this truth to actually "bear on the issues of life"—particularly, the issues that cause me to sigh with weariness and tremble with uncertainty.

When we looked at Christ's example in the last chapter, we specifically noted that He endured suffering with joyful obedience to the Father, a constant others-centeredness, and a hopeful outlook. The issues of life, however, all too often cause me to act, speak, or think in a way that is entirely contrary to this pattern. How can the provision of union with Christ change that? How does it change both the way I think and the way I act? Remember, we are seeking to be sober-minded women who think rightly about God and ourselves, for this right thinking has a direct impact on how we respond to life (i.e., what we do).

John Murray claims that there is no other truth "more suited to impart confidence and strength, comfort and joy in the Lord than this one of union with Christ."[4] Why is that so? Though we could form a large list of reasons, there are three specific aspects of our union with Christ I would like to mention in light of our declared mission to be women who are ever looking unto Jesus and thus looking to the future without fear. In Christ the believer is given the promises of *conformity*, *compassion*, and *completion*.

The Promise of Conformity

Remember the worsening nerve pain I mentioned in chapter 3? Several weeks ago, we finally got an answer to what is causing the pain: a plum-sized tumor in my leg is putting pressure on one of my nerves.

---

4. Murray, *Redemption Accomplished and Applied*, 171.

The tumor is benign and somewhat anticipated, as NF2 can result in tumors growing just about anywhere in the body. The neurologist informed us that while surgery is an option, it would come with the risk of numbness, weakness, and increased pain. Like most people, I use my legs each day—a lot. The thought of a surgery causing my leg to stop functioning or of having worse pain is enough to convince me that surgery is not the preferable option at this point. For now, we've decided to simply monitor the tumor and wait to see if it grows. I'm thankful to have an answer. But answers are not necessarily solutions, and in many cases they are simply a new breeding ground for worry or fear about things to come.

As the nerve pain has worsened in the past couple of years, it has exposed not only the weakness of my body but also the weakness of my holiness. Just like marriage and motherhood, ongoing physical pain does wonders to reveal the remaining sin that lurks within. Our trials and suffering are not always the *result* of sin, but they almost always *reveal* sin. More than I would like to admit, those times of pain have left me quick-tempered and irritable with my family. They have revealed a heart of spiritual dullness and misplaced affections when I quickly turn to anything but Scripture, such as mindless Facebook scrolling, to distract myself from the pain. Of course the exposing of our own sin in the midst of trial only adds to the misery. The suffering itself is miserable, but along with that is the disappointing reminder of my own lack of Christlike character. It's no wonder Paul said that "we who are in this tent groan, being burdened, not because we want to be unclothed, but further clothed" (2 Cor. 5:4)— clothed with a final, glorified body that is wholly untouched by both suffering and sin.

This newly discovered tumor is not currently life-threatening and, all things considered, hardly the worst news imaginable. But as long as surgery is out of the picture, the pain is probably not going anywhere. Therefore, the realistic prospect of chronic pain is discouraging not only because of the pain itself but also because of the sin that pain is bound to expose. How many times will I snap back at my boys and wish they would leave me alone? Will they grow up remembering a poor example and lack of graciousness in response to suffering? What if the pain grows more frequent and my desire for the word of God less frequent? What if life gets harder and my heart colder?

My union with Christ confronts these questions with the precious promise of *conformity*—that, for the remainder of this earthly life, the Spirit will be daily at work in me, causing me to be "transformed into the same image from one degree of glory to another" (2 Cor. 3:18 ESV). The good news of the gospel is not merely that I am united to Christ but more so the inevitable results of that union—specifically, my real participation in the death and resurrection of Christ, which Paul writes of: "Or do you not know that as many of us as were baptized into Christ Jesus were baptized into His death? Therefore we were buried with Him through baptism into death, that just as Christ was raised from the dead by the glory of the Father, even so we also should walk in newness of life" (Rom. 6:3–4).

In a way we cannot fully comprehend, believers are united to Christ in His death and resurrection. The reason we are no longer slaves of sin is because, being crucified with Christ, sin has lost its power to dominate our lives. Likewise, because we partake of His resurrection power, we gain power to walk in "newness of life" (Rom. 6:4). In Christ we are new creations with a new bent toward holiness. Barrett writes, "Just as certainly as believers partake of what Christ achieved by His atoning death, so they partake of all the victory of His glorious resurrection."[5]

Every day the Holy Spirit not only sustains my union with the risen Christ but applies to me the sanctifying benefits of that union, making me more and more like the person of Christ. And as that Spirit causes me to gaze on the risen Christ and better understand the effects of His redemptive work, I increasingly come to know, love, imitate, and obey Him.

There are many ways the Spirit powerfully works to sanctify us. Not surprisingly, Scripture teaches us that earthly suffering of all

5. Barrett, *Complete in Him*, 100.

kinds is undoubtedly one of God's chosen means to produce growth and maturity in His children: "My brethren, count it all joy when you fall into various trials, knowing that the testing of your faith produces patience" (James 1:2–3). Likewise, Paul tells us that "tribulation produces perseverance; and perseverance, character; and character, hope" (Rom. 5:3–4).

The trials of life are a help, not a hindrance, toward holiness—but this is true only for those who are united to Christ. Everyone suffers in one way or another, both believers and unbelievers. But only believers have reason to rejoice in their earthly sufferings. Those outside of Christ are spiritually dead in sin (Eph. 2:1) and separated from Him. They are not being transformed into the image of Christ day by day but are rather dominated by the power of sin. They are not being helped toward holiness in their suffering, and one day the difficulties of this earthly life will appear small compared to the horror of their eternal torment. This is not the case for the believer. Why not? Because when we are united to Christ by the Spirit, "our lives are no longer determined by what Adam has done, but by what Christ Jesus has done."[6] Our union with the One who conquered sin transfers us into an entirely new realm wherein our lives are no longer going from one degree of sin to another but rather from one degree of holiness to another.

This truth wonderfully encourages us to laugh at the days to come because it has implications for both present suffering and prospective suffering. As I have already said, some of us may now be in a season of suffering and the future may only appear bleaker. But some of us are in a season of relative ease and are anxious about what suffering may be just around the corner. You may see yourself in both camps to some degree, as I do. On the one hand, there is the present trial of nerve pain and the likelihood that as the tumor grows, surgery will eventually be necessary. On the other hand, as I said in chapter 4, I have grown somewhat "comfortable" in the challenges of NF2, and this leaves me wondering if there is a new, worse trial

6. Ferguson, *Holy Spirit*, 110.

up ahead. Whatever camp you find yourself in, we are all wondering the same thing—what if I don't have what it takes to glorify God
in future suffering? What if I fail miserably and my suffering looks
nothing like that of Christ?

And yet the promise of conformity compels us to laugh. Life
may indeed get harder, but the Spirit of Christ in us is indeed making us holier—day by day, week by week, month by month, year by
year—through both seasons of problems and seasons of prosperity.
The Spirit of Christ is sanctifying us now in ways that will better
prepare us to face the trials of tomorrow. This does not mean that
future trials will be a walk in the park. No matter how mature we are
five years from now, we will still have much to learn about following
in the footsteps of the Suffering Servant. God will go on sanctifying
us then just as He is now. But this does mean we ought to anticipate
the joy of witnessing how the Spirit has been at work in our lives,
teaching, preparing, and equipping us for whatever is down the road.
Come what may, we look to the future and anticipate not the increasing misery of sin but the increasing miracle of steadfastness.

The Promise of Compassion

Throughout the trial of my hearing loss, the Lord used many people to pray for me, speak kind words, and show me love in tangible
ways. I appreciated those people greatly and the ways God used
them to bring sincere comfort. And yet I am not surprised that the
person whose compassion meant the most to me was my dad. He
was the one person who really understood what I was going through
because he had walked through the very same thing. It wasn't that
the compassion and care of others was ungenuine or unhelpful, but
the position my dad had was unique. I didn't need to explain to him
what it was like to have four strange sounds buzzing in my ears—he
was well acquainted with the same tiresome annoyance of tinnitus.
He did not question why I didn't want to attend this or that social
gathering because he didn't want to go either.

One thing that makes the trials of life harder is when we feel as
though no one else could possibly understand what we are going

through. We take great comfort in meeting and fellowshipping
with people who have experienced similar hardships. For example,
there is a group of ladies at my church who meet on a regular basis.
They are all mothers of children with special needs, and they share
a unique bond because they are able to compassionately identify
with the many challenges of parenting a child who is different in
some way.

Isn't that what we long for? We appreciate when people are kind,
but we would love for them to feel what it's like to actually walk in
our shoes for a week. We wonder, *Is there anyone who really understands?* And if we know someone who does understand, our heart
bears a peculiar affection toward that person. We naturally show
them compassion and take comfort in knowing they will show us
the same.

This very compassion is promised to us in our union with Christ.
The writer of Hebrews comforts us with this truth: "For we do not
have a High Priest who cannot sympathize with our weaknesses, but
was in all points tempted as we are, yet without sin. Let us therefore
come boldly to the throne of grace, that we may obtain mercy and
find grace to help in time of need" (4:15–16).

As our High Priest, Jesus stood in the gap to offer a perfect
sacrifice—Himself—and thus reconcile us to a holy God whose
wrath would otherwise be on us. This is good news! Our sin has
been atoned for, and we are on our way to eternal glory. But almost
immediately we are confronted with the stark reminder that we
are not yet there. We are still in a fallen world that presents us with
daily conflicts.

The above passage in Hebrews confronts us in our discouragement with the sweet reminder that we have a High Priest who not
only saves us but identifies with us. Because He came as a man and
possessed a real human nature, He understands what it's like to live
in a world in which the body grows weary, relationships grow cold,
and temptations grow stronger. Therefore, He is not a stranger to the
many circumstances that cause us to sigh, and He sympathizes with
us as we groan in our earthly tents.

The King James Version of verse 15 reads, "For we have not an high priest which cannot be touched with the feeling of our infirmities." In a sermon on this passage, Charles Spurgeon spoke of Christ's compassion with helpful eloquence:

> He is not only touched with the feeling of the heroic endurance of the martyrs, but He sympathizes with those of us who are not heroes, but can only plead, "the spirit, indeed, is willing, but the flesh is weak." While you are entreating the Lord, thrice, to take away the thorn in the flesh, He is sympathizing with you! Is it not well that it does not say, touched with the feeling of our *patience?* our *self-denial,* our *valor?* but "with a feeling of our *infirmities*"; that is, our weakness, our littleness, the points in which we are not strong nor happy. Our pain, our depression, our trembling, our sensitiveness; He is touched with these though He falls not into the sin which so often comes of them. Hold fast this truth of God, for it may greatly tend to your consolation some day.[7]

This is the Christ to whom we are intimately united. He is not just our High Priest but our husband. He desires intimacy with us, and how much more eagerly do we pursue this intimacy and closeness when we realize His tender and sympathetic heart toward us.

When my husband and I got married, there were still many things we didn't know about each other. I didn't know I was marrying a man who sleeps like a rock, does not like potatoes, and is fantastically ticklish in his feet. He didn't know he was marrying a woman who washes and reuses Ziploc bags, loves bean burritos, and enjoys reading about politics. These discoveries have been trivial, but over the years we have also come to discover more significant things about one another, including particular weaknesses, sorrows, and sin struggles. More than once my husband has endured a very discouraged wife who is distressed by her lack of freedom to fellowship with ease in group settings. And many times has my husband

---

7. Charles H. Spurgeon, "The Tenderness of Jesus," in *The Metropolitan Tabernacle Pulpit* (Edinburgh: Banner of Truth, 1970), 36:319–20.

endured the sting of his wife's irritability and selfishness toward him. At times I have wondered how he does not grow weary of me or why he doesn't throw his hands up and cry, "Really? This, *again*?" Instead, he is gentle, quick to forgive, and faithful in prayer for the growth of my soul. I fail often as a wife and am sometimes slow to overcome the challenges of life, but I am never long without the comfort that my marriage remains, and my husband loves and accepts me. This comfort is not gained by looking at my marriage certificate or wedding album. This comfort is gained by the friendship and intimacy I share with my husband and his readiness to extend that to me.

So it is in my union with Christ. As my sympathetic High Priest and husband, He does not grow weary of me. Rather than throwing in the towel and abandoning His distressed and sorrowful beloved, He remains. His Spirit continues to dwell in me. He understands what it's like to suffer greatly, for He Himself suffered much. And because I am united to Him, there is a real sense in which He truly does suffer through the same things I suffer. When Christ called out to Saul on the road to Damascus, He said, "Saul, why are you persecuting *Me*?" (Acts 9:4, emphasis added). Saul was inflicting great suffering on Christ's beloved people, but it was as though he was persecuting Christ Himself (v. 5).

Christ compassionately identifies with us not only in our suffering but also in our temptation to sin. Christ was truly tempted. This is hard for us to understand because we must also declare that Christ was entirely sinless. It's helpful to understand what temptation is. Temptation presents us with a path that is *other than the path of obedience and righteousness*. We are presented with these wrong paths from both without (Satan and the world) and within (our own sinful desires), and the result is that we often fail to resist disobedience and are instead swayed by the lusts of our flesh. Christ too was presented with many paths that were other than the path of obedience. These temptations did not come from within because He did not have indwelling sin. Rather, these temptations came from without and preyed on His human nature. For example, when Christ was in the wilderness being tempted by Satan, He was hungry (a natural

result of being human) and was presented with a path of disobedience that would cure that hunger. He resisted the temptation. And
every other time Christ was presented with a path that was other than
His Father's will—a pain-free path, a conflict-free path, a cross-free
path—He resisted the temptation and chose the path of obedience.

At times we are prone to declare Christ's compassion insufficient
or illegitimate because He didn't know what it was like to sin. He
knew what it was to suffer, but He didn't know the many miseries of
sin intermingling with that suffering. But we must remember that if
Christ could identify with us in our sin, He would not be a Savior.
The compassion He extends as He identifies with us in our affliction is indeed comforting, but all the more so because He *cannot*
identify with us in our sin. He is tender and patient toward sinners not because He excuses sin but because He has made a way of
escape from sin. He does not come alongside us in our sin and say,
"Don't worry, I failed too." He comes to us in our weak and miserable
defeat and says, "Get up, beloved. I died for this, and I refuse to leave
you here!"

The Promise of Completion

Our union with Christ, His Spirit dwelling in us, gives us the promise of conformity, compassion, and finally, completion. We will look
briefly at this final point and return to a similar theme in the final
chapter. Perhaps the simplest way of putting this promise is that once
we are united to Christ, we are united to Him forever. We are in
a union that cannot be broken. We laugh at the days to come not
because of the *potential* that Christ will never leave us or forsake us,
but because we are *promised* He will never leave us or forsake us.
Paul tells us that nothing—things present nor things to come—can
separate us from the love of Christ (Rom. 8:38–39). Nothing. The
sorrow of our affliction and the misery of our sin may at times tempt
us to think that Christ has deserted us or grown disgusted with us.
It is in those moments that we must be sober-minded and align our
thoughts with Scripture.

Paul encourages the Philippians, "And I am sure of this, that he who began a good work in you will bring it to completion at the day of Jesus Christ" (Phil. 1:6 ESV). God finishes what He starts in His elect and does not fail to bring them home. And let us be reminded of what Peter wrote: "Therefore gird up the loins of your mind, be sober, and rest your hope fully upon the grace that is to be brought to you at the revelation of Jesus Christ" (1 Peter 1:13). In other words, "Think rightly and steadfastly about the glorious truth I've set before you and in doing so, confidently expect that when Christ returns the Father will declare, 'She is His!' and welcome you to your eternal home." The grace that *was* given in our justification and *is* given in our sanctification *will be* given at our glorification.

And what is the glorious reality Peter had set before his readers? What truth would compel them to rejoice in their present suffering and confidently expect a day to come when Christ would welcome them home? "Blessed be the God and Father of our Lord Jesus Christ, who according to His abundant mercy has begotten us again to a living hope through the resurrection of Jesus Christ from the dead, to an inheritance incorruptible and undefiled and that does not fade away, reserved in heaven for you, who are kept by the power of God through faith for salvation ready to be revealed in the last time" (1 Peter 1:3–5).

Peter says that those who have been born again have the hope (confident expectation) of a future inheritance. As his readers would have been prone to set their minds on difficult things that may happen in the future, he wants them to instead set their minds on the things that will happen in the future. Thus he describes their hope as *living*—undying, permanent, ongoing—and their inheritance as *incorruptible*, one that will never fade away. *Future suffering is potential—it may happen. Future salvation is promised—it will happen.*

But what if our suffering and sin grow so intense, so seemingly hopeless, that we fully and finally fall away? How can we be sure we'll make it home? We can be sure because in light of our union with Christ, we are already there. Romans 6 tells us we share in Christ's death and resurrection. Paul's epistle to the Ephesians takes that thought further and tells us the astounding truth that we also share in Christ's eternal reign in the heavenly places. The same power that did not leave Christ in the grave but raised Him up and seated Him at the Father's right hand is the same power that "made us alive together with Christ…and raised us up together, and made us sit together in the heavenly places in Christ Jesus" (Eph. 2:5–6; cf. Eph. 1:19–20). In God's eyes, our eternal destination is as good as done.

And God wants us to be convinced of this wonderful reality as well. If my union with Christ promised me conformity to holiness and compassion in weakness but no certainty of that union's permanence, my laughter would be short-lived. Life would be a constant walking on eggshells, a fearful and constant questioning of whether Christ was still devoted to me or whether I had done something to turn Him away. But my union with Christ is not dominated by fear because Christ's Spirit dwelling in me is, as Paul says, "the Spirit of adoption by whom we cry out, 'Abba, Father'" (Rom. 8:15). These are the same words Christ prayed in the garden of Gethsemane. In great distress over the cup of wrath He would soon drink, He humbly and heroically submitted Himself to the Father's will. In our union with Christ, the Spirit bears witness to our hearts that as children of God and heirs with Christ, we may call on this same sovereign, loving Father. Do God's children suffer? This side of heaven, yes—often in great measure. But as they suffer alongside Christ while submitting to their Father's will, they do so with the confident expectation that they will "also be glorified with him" (Rom. 8:17 ESV).

Today we may grow tired, and tomorrow we may shed great tears. But even so, the sound of laughter may be faintly heard on our lips when we realize that in Christ we have been given a father. And one day we will be with Him forever—for no one can snatch us out of His hand.

Part 3

Laughter: Its Doing

As obedient children, do not be conformed to the passions of your former ignorance, but as he who called you is holy, you also be holy in all your conduct, since it is written, "You shall be holy, for I am holy."

—1 PETER 1:14–16 ESV

Nine

HER PRAYERS
The Humble Expectation of a Daughter

> Prayer is the fruition of adoption, for it brings to full expression the desire of adopted children for the honor of their Father's name, their longing for the expansion of His kingdom among men, and their holy resolve to submit to His will.
>
> —Joel R. Beeke, *Taking Hold of God: Reformed and Puritan Perspectives on Prayer*

Earlier this week I was in the kitchen finishing lunch cleanup. Usually by this time of day, my boys have lots of pent-up energy that comes out in the form of running around, wrestling, and probably a lot of noise (there are perks to being deaf). When I walked into the dining area to wipe the table, I was not happy with what I found: remnants of a hard-boiled egg scattered on the hallway rug, the hardwood floor, and the sofa in the adjoining living room. "Boys! Who did this?" I asked with clear disapproval. Part of my frustration was that it was already a very busy day, and cleaning up a strewn-about hard-boiled egg was not on my to-do list. But the other part of my frustration was that they knew better—my four-year-old knew better than to throw an egg around, and my six-year-old knew better than to laugh at him for doing so.

As their mother, my goal is not simply that my children would know and understand what is true, right, and appropriate. I want them to learn how to act on that knowledge in daily life. I can teach them all the dos and don'ts of table manners, toy sharing, and personal hygiene, but that is only half my job. I must help them to actually apply this information to their daily life by giving correction, reminders, and appropriate discipline.

Likewise, the Christian life is not a life of mere knowing, but one of *doing*. We learn the truth so that we might live in light of the truth. We value the articulation and study of doctrine not for the purpose of feeding our pride, but that we might increasingly discern how our daily lives ought to reflect those truths. In our pursuit to smile at the present and laugh at the future, we reflect on how the truths we know ought to affect the way we respond to the trials, confusion, and burdens of life.

Unfortunately, increasing knowledge of God's word and sound thinking do not automatically result in right living. If that were the case, Paul's epistles would be half their size. When Paul wrote his letters, he clearly had equal concern for doctrine and doing, and therefore he gave time and attention to both: (1) *This is what you ought to know and believe about God and the gospel*; and (2) *this is how you ought to live in light of those truths.* This is why Paul urges the Ephesians to "walk worthy" of their calling after laying before them the profound truths of the gospel (Eph. 4:1). He wants them to be sure that their lives do not contradict the doctrine they claim to believe.

Peter had this same concern for his readers. We have already noted in an earlier chapter that the book of 1 Peter could be summed up as an epistle of hope. But let's add something to that: the hope Peter desired his readers to cultivate was *a hope that would produce holiness*. Not only were they to have a sober-minded hope toward the future but they were to do so as "obedient children, not conforming to the former lusts" (1:14). He continued, "But as He who called you is holy, you also be holy in all your conduct, because it is written, 'Be holy, for I am holy.' And if you call on the Father, who without partiality judges according to each one's work, conduct yourselves throughout the time of your stay here in fear" (vv. 15–17).

If we are thinking rightly about Christ's work in the past and rejoicing in the resulting inheritance that is to be ours in the future, we cannot be ignorant about the way we are living in the present. If we would be women who know the gospel and thus laugh at the days to come, we must be women who know the gospel and thus take thought for the day at hand. We must examine our lives and ask ourselves whether our hope-filled doctrine is shaping our daily doing.

Thus far, we have caught a vision for the woman who laughs at the days to come and examined some of the gospel truths that shape her laughter. In these final three chapters, I would like to look at three specific areas of doing in the life of a sober-minded woman who laughs at the days to come: her *prayers*, her *participation*, and her *prospect*. There is a lot more to holiness of life than these three areas. But I have chosen these three in parallel to the examples of Christ we looked at in chapter 7, and I believe they are particularly relevant for the woman who pursues a life of laughter. How, then, does she pray?

A Decade of Disappointment

I don't know exactly how many people have prayed for my hearing to be restored, but the answer is *a lot*. From the time I began losing it, God continually chose to put people in my path who were entirely convinced that I was going to be healed. This resulted in some interesting occasions. One time I was anointed with oil—a Styrofoam cup filled nearly to the brim with oil—while a group of people fervently asked (more like demanded) God to heal me. That same night someone was convinced they were supposed to keep their fingers in my ears while we waited to see if God would answer our prayers.

As I already mentioned, I was among those who were entirely convinced. One time I felt I needed to really get serious about praying for healing and decided to go on a two-week fast. On the morning of the third day, I was quite weak and ended up passing out in the shower. Hours later I came home from the emergency room with stitches in my forehead and a load of discouragement. A few years later, my friend and I pulled an all-nighter in prayer, wondering if our unrelenting audacity would finally be rewarded.

There is one incident that is especially memorable to me, equally strange and dear in retrospect. I was attending a small discipleship school where, to my delight, both the leaders and students enthusiastically rallied around me and prayed fervently and expectantly for healing. One week the men put their heads together and decided they would begin taking turns "interceding" for me each day by wearing a pair of noise-canceling headphones. Under the headphones they would wear a pair of small earphones connected to an MP3 player, listening to a continuous track of strange sounds that were supposed to mimic my tinnitus. After the headphones had made it through all the guys, the girls joined in and started taking turns. This went on into the next semester, when a new group of students arrived and they began taking turns.

The semester ended, and many fervent prayers had not been answered. But then something quite exciting happened. A smaller group of students remained on campus in between semesters, and it was during this time that one of the men felt God was leading him to devote a significant amount of his time to private prayer. He was convinced that God had told him to put on the headphones and pray for me *until* I was healed. *Surely, this is it,* I thought. *God has been leading me to this very season of life, and we are on the brink of witnessing a miracle!* After all, how long would God let him wear those ridiculous-looking, uncomfortable headphones?

A long time, it turned out. This zealous student's name was Nick, and he wore those ugly green headphones for 222 days, only taking them off to shower, sleep, and drive. During those months he prayed, and prayed, and prayed—in the rain, in the middle of the night, alone in his room, and sometimes with fasting. Life was full of anticipation, as we believed the healing was just around the corner.

At the end of 222 days, in an unexpected turn of events, we decided it was time for the headphones to come off. A group of students assembled with one of the leaders, and after a brief explanation, Nick's poor ears were finally free. I felt the tension—a celebratory relief that Nick could hear again and the devastating letdown that I could not. I held my peace in those moments but later on wept freely behind closed doors.

That season of the headphones was one of much solitude for Nick, and when he wasn't praying for my healing, he was often reading and studying his Bible. It was during that time he began to discover a God whose evident sovereignty was difficult to reckon with. Through His word, God was slowly but surely beginning to challenge Nick's thinking, and after a while he started to seriously question some of his doctrine. As if things couldn't get even more complicated, he was also falling in love with the girl he was praying for. And as you may have guessed, this is the same Nick I fell in love with and to whom I am now married.

Both of our middle names mean "God is gracious"—and that is exactly what He was and has been to us. Gently and patiently, He brought us to a sounder understanding of His word and what His children are promised in the gospel. What had we believed wrongly? Were we wrong to believe that God still heals? Were we wrong to believe in the power of prayer? Were we wrong to believe that God would be glorified through a healing? No, we firmly believe that God can and does do miracles today. We believe that prayer is powerful and a means He often ordains to bring about those miracles. And we believe that earthly manifestations of His sovereign power are indeed an opportunity for Him to be glorified.

The problem was that we were *absolutely certain* of what God was going to do. We believed that Christ had purchased physical healing on the cross and that it was God's definite will for it to be manifested this side of heaven. I remember one of the leaders at the discipleship school saying one time with sincere confidence, "I *know* what God is going to do." So did we. But then He didn't do it, and that left us with a lot of questions. Was there something wrong with the way we prayed? Was there a prayer-hindering sin? Were we giving up too soon, accepting a no answer because we weren't willing to wait any longer?

God's Gracious Correction

The disappointment of not being healed was devastating and painful. The correction God gently gave us in the aftermath, however, was life-changing. Looking back, I see two major ways God corrected our error and reformed our thinking in the months that followed our wedding day. Both of these corrections have big implications for the prayers of the woman who laughs.

First, He revealed His sovereignty. This sovereignty was not just a power to heal sick bodies. This was a sovereignty that sometimes chooses to *not* heal sick bodies. I do not doubt that in our prayers we all had a sincere desire to see God glorified. And dare I say it—I believe there was an element of our persistence and expectation that was pleasing to our Father. We were believing in a big God, a kind God, a prayer-answering God—all of which He is. But rather than ultimately and humbly bowing the knee to His sovereign choice over the matter, in a sense we took pride in not taking no for an answer. As a result, there was a load of pressure on us to be praying (and living) the right way. We already knew for certain what God was going to do (so we thought), and thus much of our attention was given to what we needed to do before He would do it.

Scripture speaks with amazing simplicity: "But our God is in heaven; He does whatever He pleases" (Ps. 115:3). The expanse of God's sovereignty does not get much clearer than that. And we must keep that sovereignty stamped on our minds when we come to Him in prayer. After decades of quadriplegia and working with people who suffer in countless ways, Joni Eareckson Tada has come to a humble and hard-won conclusion: "Here is what I believe: *God reserves the right to heal or not…as He sees fit.*"[1] I wish this same conclusion had shaped our prayers years ago, but I am thankful for the clarity, contentment, and comfort it brings us today.

But why would God say no if we are asking for something we are promised in the gospel, something Christ purchased for His people? This brings me to the second way God corrected us. Through

---

1. Tada, *Place of Healing*, 41, emphasis original.

His atoning death on the cross and victorious resurrection, Christ reversed the curse of sin. This includes all the suffering, sorrow, sickness, and tragedy that go along with that sin. But here is the simple truth we had failed to understand: the glorious salvation we are given in Christ is a "now and not yet" salvation. One of the simplest ways of seeing this concept in Scripture is by looking at the different ways our salvation is described.

We *have been saved* (Eph. 2:8). Our salvation is a past event. God has regenerated us, we have believed in Christ, and God has declared us righteous in Him. The Judge has made His ruling, and the case is closed.

We *are being saved* (1 Cor. 1:18). Little by little, day by day, we are being conformed to the likeness of Christ in the lifelong process of sanctification. Sin does not rule, but it does remain, and thus we actively seek to kill it and increasingly walk in holiness.

We *will be saved* (Rom. 5:9). God's people are being guarded "for salvation ready to be revealed in the last time" (1 Peter 1:5). This is why Paul speaks of Christians putting on "as a helmet the hope of salvation" (1 Thess. 5:8). Salvation is indeed something we have already been given, but it is also something we are patiently and confidently waiting for. A day is coming when that salvation will be perfect and its application complete—no sin, no suffering, no sickness.

Before I had this "now and not yet" paradigm shift, my laughter toward the future was confined to that one imagined earthly day when my ears would be opened and the miracle complete. I smiled much as I thought about that day and wondered what special occasion God had chosen for it. Easter Sunday? The breaking of dawn after an all-night prayer session? My wedding day? Or maybe just an ordinary day, out of the blue. Who would I call first? What music would I listen to? I was consumed with waiting and praying for that uncertain earthly day rather than setting my hope on and rejoicing in that certain future day of glorification. My longing for earthly relief was great, but my longing for that final heavenly rest was greatly lacking.

Coming to this new understanding gave me the freedom to acknowledge that the earthly day of healing may never come. Though Christ has once and for all purchased full, final deliverance from the curse of the fall, we must remember that this sin-ravaged, passing-away world was never meant to be the stage on which the fullness of salvation is miraculously manifested. Not every disease will be healed. Not every temptation will be overcome. Not every relationship will be mended. Not every longing will be fulfilled—not because we aren't praying with enough faith or persistence or holiness but because we still live in a world in which the entire created order is sighing and longing to be set free from corruption and decay: "For we know that the whole creation groans and labors with birth pangs together until now. Not only that, but we also who have the firstfruits of the Spirit, even we ourselves groan within ourselves, eagerly waiting for the adoption, the redemption of our body" (Rom. 8:22–23).

These verses beautifully illustrate the concept of a "now and not yet" salvation. We presently have the down payment of the Spirit, the joy of justification, the encouragement of ongoing sanctification, and a host of other joys and benefits; and yet, even we ourselves are still groaning along with the rest of creation. Why? Because we are still waiting for the full manifestation of our inheritance as children of God; we are still waiting for redeemed bodies and a redeemed world entirely free of sin and suffering. There is a degree of completion and perfection that we have yet to attain, and we needn't be ashamed of that.

Coming to grips with these realities—God's absolute sovereignty and the "now and not yet" nature of salvation—was greatly comforting and liberating. I could not say with certainty why God had chosen to say no to such persistent, believing prayers, but there was great relief in the realization that I didn't have to. Instead of hanging my head low in defeat, I could joyfully stare God's no in the face without feeling the need to explain it.

How, Then, Does She Pray?

As encouraging as these truths were, they left me with some questions. When life presents me with a difficult circumstance, when I look to the days ahead and see the looming threat of sorrow upon sorrow, and when I know my God is powerful and able to bring about change, how do I pray in light of these truths? How can I be a sober-minded woman who believes rightly about God's sovereignty and the imperfect nature of present salvation and yet still come boldly before the throne of God with my requests? If I declare that God is absolutely sovereign over a matter, should I even be praying about it at all?

Yes, I should still be praying—that much I knew. Anyone who is the least bit familiar with Scripture would readily admit this is not debatable. The Bible is filled with both commands to pray and examples of prayer. We believe that God ordains not only the end but also the means to the end—and often He uses prayer as the means to bring about His sovereign purposes. Undoubtedly, we are to be a praying people. And therefore our response to God's sovereignty and the incomplete nature of our present salvation is not passive resignation. We submit to these truths, but not silently.

Rather, our submission to these truths is demonstrated in frequent and fervent sober-minded prayers in which we think rightly about God and self and pray accordingly. These are the prayers of the woman who laughs. She is not afraid to bring her requests before God, for in her heartfelt, earnest prayers she is ever aware that the sovereign God to whom she prays is also her Father, who cares about her smallest need.

As we saw in chapter 6, the fatherliness of God plays a big part in how we respond to His sovereignty. We saw this again in chapter 7 as we looked at the example of Jesus and His entire submission to His Father's will. This is seen most clearly in the hours leading up to Jesus's death, when He kneels to pray in the garden of Gethsemane. Jesus is absolutely submitted to the will of the Father, and yet not silently, for He comes boldly to the throne of grace and makes His request known: "O My Father, if it is possible, let this cup pass from Me; nevertheless, not as I will, but as You will" (Matt. 26:39).

In a life of laughter, we submit to the will of our sovereign Father. And though we may not know with certainty how and when He will answer our prayers, we go on praying expectantly according to what we do know. In other words, the prayer life of the woman who laughs is not one of silent submission but of *sound* submission.

What does it mean for our submission to be sound? When something is sound it is founded on truth—correct, free from error, valid, orthodox. It is not diseased and defective, but healthy and unadulterated. When we pray with sound submission, we keep a close eye on Scripture so as to be praying in harmony with what God has revealed to us—His character, His priorities, His will, and His dealings with man. D. A. Carson writes,

> Brothers and sisters in Christ, at the heart of all our praying must be a biblical vision. That vision embraces who God is, what he has done, who we are, where we are going, what we must value and cherish. That vision drives us toward increasing conformity with Jesus, toward lives lived in the light of eternity, toward hearty echoing of the church's ongoing cry, "Even so, come, Lord Jesus!" That vision must shape our prayers, so that the things that most concern us in prayer are those that concern the heart of God. Then we will persevere in our praying, until we reach the goal God himself has set for us.[2]

That is a beautiful (and challenging, yes?) summary of sound submission in prayer. With this foundation of soundness in mind, I would like to look at three specific ways this kind of submission is displayed in our prayers along with examples from the prayers we find in Scripture.

A Humble Submission

First, a sound submission is a *humble submission*. The first question of the Westminster Shorter Catechism asks, "What is the chief

---

2. D. A. Carson, *Praying with Paul: A Call to Spiritual Reformation* (Grand Rapids: Baker Academic, 2015), 43.

end of man?" Many of us are familiar with the answer: "Man's chief end is to glorify God and enjoy Him forever." The same thing could likewise be said of prayer. Praying with that end in mind (glorifying God and enjoying Him), however, requires a radical shift from our natural, human-centered thinking to God-centered thinking. It is very easy for us to approach prayer thinking primarily about our own felt needs and how God can meet those needs. Or (perhaps a little less selfish sounding), we approach prayer being persuaded of what would glorify God the most, and so we pray only for that specific outcome.

As I said, I do believe we had a sincere desire to see God glorified when we prayed for my healing. But looking back, I don't see much enjoyment of God in the way we prayed. Rather than seeing prayer as sweet communion with God, in which we delight in Him and He aligns our desires with His desires (Ps. 37:4), we saw it more as a wrestling match in which to prove our unwavering faith and persistence. Did we want to see God glorified? I think so—but only if that meant He would be glorified the way we wanted Him to be.

Let me be clear about something: it is not wrong to come to God with specific needs and desires. The problem is when we become utterly convinced of what God's will is and refuse to be still until we see that very thing come about. Of course, we can (and should) be utterly convinced of God's will when we are praying for something His word has clearly promised (more on that soon). But many of the things we are so quick to pray for are not things that are specifically promised to us in Scripture. Here are a few examples:

- We are not promised that this winter our kids will be entirely sickness free.

- We are not promised that our house will sell in record time and for the price we desire.

- We are not promised that all our children will be saved at a young age and walk faithfully with God the rest of their days.

- We are not promised trial-free marriages to spouses who will never fall into sin.

- And we are definitely not promised a life free from fender benders, broken washing machines, and temper tantrums.

Is it okay to pray about these things? Yes, but when our chief end is to glorify God and enjoy Him, our prayers will take on a humble disposition in which we bow our knee to the supremely wise One and echo the words of Christ: "Your will be done" (Matt. 26:42).

In this humble submission we will be quick to acknowledge that first we need God to give us a desire for Him to be glorified. If we are honest, God's glory is often far from our minds when we begin to pray about a need. And even when we do sincerely have that desire, it is something that always ought to be increasing. And second, we will acknowledge that sometimes God is glorified when He gives, and sometimes He is glorified when He takes away. And thus we will unashamedly end our prayers with the words "Your will be done"—not because our faith is small but because we are small and acknowledge that God's ways are higher than our ways.

Job was a man who learned how to approach God with humble submission. After God takes away his children and all his possessions, Job falls to the ground in worship and utters these astonishing words:

> Naked I came from my mother's womb,
> And naked shall I return there.
> The LORD gave, and the LORD has taken away;
> Blessed be the name of the LORD. (Job 1:21)

God was God and Job was not—that much he knew. But throughout the next several chapters, we see Job having a difficult time understanding God's ways (his friends, by the way, are no help). There doesn't seem to be a valid explanation for his suffering. God does not resolve this by giving Job a clear, detailed explanation of why He did what He did. Rather, God gives Job a magnificent vision of who He is—an all-powerful, all-knowing, all-wise God who is worthy of all praise, honor, and glory. If you want a very edifying glimpse of this God, read chapters 38–41 in one sitting. What is Job's response?

> I know that You can do everything,
> And that no purpose of Yours can be withheld from You.

You asked, "Who is this who hides counsel without
   knowledge?"
Therefore I have uttered what I did not understand,
Things too wonderful for me, which I did not know....

I have heard of You by the hearing of the ear,
But now my eye sees You.
Therefore I abhor myself,
And repent in dust and ashes. (Job 42:2-3, 5-6)

Job is not able to explain why God allowed him to suffer. But when
he sees the greatness of God, he realizes he doesn't need an explanation, for he now understands that the chief end of his life—and thus
the chief end of his prayers—is to know, enjoy, and glorify this God
forever, in both the day of prosperity and the day of great loss.

An Honest Submission

Second, a sound submission is an *honest submission*. It is easy to
understand why the book of Psalms is one we so quickly turn to
when we are facing something stressful or difficult, whether it be
as big as a cancer diagnosis or as small as a week buried in sibling
squabbles and interrupted schedules. The Psalms are full of raw
emotions and difficult circumstances we can easily relate to. Here are
a few examples:

> *Loneliness*
> Turn Yourself to me, and have mercy on me,
> For I am desolate [isolated, abandoned] and afflicted. (25:16)

> *Grief*
> For my life is spent with grief,
> And my years with sighing;
> My strength fails because of my iniquity,
> And my bones waste away. (31:10)

> *Discouragement and turmoil*
> Why are you cast down, O my soul?
> And why are you disquieted within me? (42:5)

Shame
My dishonor is continually before me,
And the shame of my face has covered me. (44:15)

Desire
LORD, You have heard the desire of the humble;
You will prepare their heart;
You will cause Your ear to hear. (10:17)

Brokenheartedness
The LORD is near to those who have a broken heart. (34:18)

Pain
Look on my affliction and my pain,
And forgive all my sins. (25:18)

Confession of sin
I acknowledged my sin to You,
And my iniquity I have not hidden.
I said, "I will confess my transgressions to the LORD,"
And You forgave the iniquity of my sin. (32:5)

Weariness and weeping
I am weary with my groaning;
All night I make my bed swim;
I drench my couch with my tears. (6:6)

God did not create us to respond to the ups and downs of life as
indifferent robots. We were created with a great capacity to feel and
express emotion. These emotions are not sinful, and we are free to
bring them to God in prayer. Indeed, the woman who laughs at the
days to come will also be a woman who weeps freely in God's presence. Our submission to Him is not stoicism or, worse, a fake smile
while we pretend everything is fine. God can handle our emotions,
and as a father He is not unsympathetic toward us. When my six-
year-old falls off his bike and badly scrapes his knee, do I chide him
for his tears and push him away when he comes crying to me? Do
I roll my eyes when he tells me that riding a bike is too hard and he
never wants to get on it again? No, I let him sit on my lap, wipe away

his tears, and put a bandage on his knee. I won't allow him to give up and put his bike in the basement, but I also won't get angry if there are additional tears and scraped knees throughout the summer.

Honest submission is one way we can learn how to commune with God and enjoy Him in prayer. The Psalms paint a picture of one who is simply sitting before heaven's throne, with no hurry to go anywhere. When we are honest with God in prayer, we are not just dropping by with a few quick requests, but coming to seek intimacy with Him. True intimacy requires honesty and vulnerability. It also requires knowledge and understanding. A marriage will not consist of much intimacy if the husband and wife never spend time together, never share their feelings with each other, and never seek to observe and discover new things about each other.

David's prayers are a wonderful comfort to us, and we would do well to refer to them for help in forming our own honest prayers. But there is more to honesty than sharing with God how we are feeling and the trials we are facing. Part of having an honest submission in prayer is being honest about who God is. And we see this expressed in the Psalms just as much as, if not more than, descriptions of human emotion and difficulty:

For You are not a God who takes pleasure in wickedness,
Nor shall evil dwell with You. (5:4)

Oh, taste and see that the LORD is good;
Blessed is the man who trusts in Him! (34:8)

You will show me the path of life;
In Your presence is fullness of joy;
At Your right hand are pleasures forevermore. (16:11)

The LORD is my rock and my fortress and my deliverer;
My God, my strength, in whom I will trust;
My shield and the horn of my salvation, my stronghold. (18:2)

Behold, the eye of the LORD is on those who fear Him,
On those who hope in His mercy. (33:18)

> For the LORD God is a sun and shield;
> The LORD will give grace and glory;
> No good thing will He withhold
> From those who walk uprightly. (84:11)

These verses are a mere tip of the iceberg in the Psalms, and there are many, many more that confront our questioning, quiet our fears, and comfort us in our sorrow. We need not disregard or hide our emotions—but we do need to deal with those emotions in a way that glorifies and honors God. And one of the best ways to do that is by being quick to declare what is true about Him. When this kind of honesty marks our fervent prayers, our weeping will give way to worship and our confusion to confident expectation.

A Hopeful Submission

Third, a sound submission is a *hopeful submission*. One of the reasons why it was so hard not to be healed was because we had been so certain it was going to happen. Not getting something is one thing, but not getting something you really hoped for is quite another thing. Every year at Christmastime when my mother-in-law asks for a list of gift ideas, my husband often asks for a set of books to add to his ever-growing library. One year he put two different options on his list, and since those were the only ideas he offered, he was quite certain his mom would purchase one of them.

When it came time for us to open our gifts, he noticed there was nothing under the tree that resembled a box of books. And when it was his turn to open a gift, he was handed a package the size of a shoebox. He unwrapped the gift and found a very nice pair of running shoes. His mom put on a smile and made a comment about the shoes being his "big gift" that year. As grateful as Nick was for the running shoes, he couldn't help but feel a twinge (okay, maybe a load) of disappointment that he hadn't received a set of books. There were a lot of other things Nick had not received that year; he did not receive a new car, a gift card to his favorite restaurant, a suit jacket, or a year's supply of ice cream. No doubt he would have loved to receive any of those things! But he was not expecting to receive them, and that made all the difference—there was no disappointment that he did not.

Nick tried hard not to show his disappointment, and the gift-opening went on. A few minutes later, his mom brought out one more gift that she had hidden—a box of books. We look back on that Christmas and laugh, but I think it perfectly illustrates that whether or not we hoped for something impacts the measure of joy we have in receiving it. And when we don't receive what we hoped for, we feel a sense of disappointment we wouldn't otherwise feel if we had never asked for it in the first place.

If our submission to God in prayer is sound (i.e., in alignment with God's word), it will also be a hopeful submission because we will be praying for and expecting things that God has promised. God does not lie:

> God is not a man, that He should lie,
> Nor a son of man, that He should repent.
> Has He said, and will He not do?
> Or has He spoken, and will He not make it good?
> (Num. 23:19)

God keeps His promises; our job is to go to Scripture and find out what those promises are.

Does God promise in His word that we will be healed of all sickness and disease this side of heaven? I do not believe He does. And as I noted above, there are many other specific things that we are not promised. Just because we are not promised these things doesn't mean we should never pray for them. God is able to heal diseases, soften the hardened hearts of children, mend broken marriages, and even orchestrate the traffic on the highway so that we are not late for an appointment. And when He does give us these good gifts, He does not do it begrudgingly, but as a father who delights to give good gifts to his children.

The trap we are prone to fall into is banking all our prayers and hopes on something that we are not promised while neglecting to acknowledge and pray for the things we are promised. We are promised that "all things work together for good to those who love God, to those who are the called according to His purpose" (Rom. 8:28). What is that "good"? Comfort? Convenience? Health and wealth? Obedient children? Actually, the "good" Paul is referring to is our conformity to Christ, our holiness, as seen in verse 29. And this is the highest good God could promise us because growth in holiness means growth in knowing the Father, treasuring Christ and our union with Him, and submitting cheerfully to the Spirit. And when we are growing in those things, we will inevitably be growing in joy. As we saw in the last chapter, we are also promised that God will complete our sanctification and bring us home to glory.

Perhaps this is why Paul's prayers in his epistles are largely focused on holiness in the present and hope toward the future. Though many of the recipients of his letters were going through various trials (e.g., persecution, false teachers, church conflict), we don't find him praying they would be delivered from those circumstances. Instead, he prays they would abound in love for one another (Phil. 1:9), grow in knowledge and discernment (Phil. 1:9), know the hope to which they were called (Eph. 1:18), have strength to comprehend the love of Christ (Eph. 3:19), be filled with the knowledge of God's will (Col. 1:9), and walk in joyful patience and endurance (Col. 1:11).

Paul was not afraid to ask God to remove the thorn in his flesh—he pleaded with God to remove it. But its removal was not something He could claim was promised to him in God's word. And that is why he was not crushed when God's answer to his request was no. Instead, he turned his hope toward the power of Christ resting on him in his weaknesses, whereby Paul would be sanctified and God would be glorified.

Ten

HER PARTICIPATION
The Selfless Love of a Sister

Let us hold fast the confession of our hope without waver-
ing, for He who promised is faithful. And let us consider one
another in order to stir up love and good works, not forsaking
the assembling of ourselves together, as is the manner of some,
but exhorting one another, and so much the more as you see
the Day approaching.

—Hebrews 10:23–25

When my husband and I moved from Colorado to Ohio in our first
year of marriage, one of our main priorities was to find a biblical
church where we could become active members. I can still remember that first morning we visited Heritage Reformed Baptist Church.
The pastor had recently begun preaching through the book of John,
and by the end of his sermon my husband had a wide-eyed look on
his face that read, "Wow—*that* was preaching!"

In the weeks that followed, we continued to be struck by the
pastor's obvious commitment to preach the word of God with
depth, soundness, and clarity. But as I observed the families of this
church—particularly the women—I was also struck by their commitment to show up in the first place. By all means, there was nothing
externally appealing about the church. The building was small and
plain. The half-hour break after Sunday school consisted of Folgers
coffee and a crowded hallway. The nursery was full of outdated toys,
and the nursing mothers' room could be accessed only by walking

up a steep stairway—not the easiest thing to do when you're carrying a newborn and a bulging diaper bag.

Nevertheless, I noticed something: these ladies wanted to be at church. Some of them had four, seven, or eleven children. Some of them drove thirty minutes to get there. Some of them were single or childless and were forced to be reminded of that again, as they were surrounded by happy families. Some of them were exhausted from a week of homeschooling, health issues, or parenting challenges (or maybe all three). But no matter what they had faced in the previous six days of life in a fallen world, they woke up on Sunday morning knowing what they would be doing that day: worshiping God and fellowshipping with His people. Children were fed and dressed, shoes were retrieved, and slow cookers were loaded into minivans. Evening services and Wednesday-night prayer meetings were similar, minus the slow cookers. People showed up—not because it was easy or convenient but because they were committed to participating in corporate worship with God's people.

The example of those brothers and sisters was encouraging but also convicting, as I saw my own lack of enthusiasm toward Sundays. I didn't mind going to the evening services, and spending a chunk of time on Saturday preparing food for Sunday's potluck wasn't the end of the world. The difficulty was that the entire day required listening—to the praising, the praying, the preaching, and the people. Indeed, the ability to hear was useful on Sundays, and I had spent nearly a decade and a half trying to figure out how to do church without it.

There is more to the Christian life than public worship. God has also given us the private means of grace, such as prayer and reading of the word. Going through a prolonged season of suffering was a wonderful opportunity to grow through those means. The years I struggled through hearing loss were some of the most spiritually formative of my life, and I have the stacks of journals to prove it. I am thankful for that growth and the way God used that season to draw me closer to Him.

But growth in private worship can never be a replacement for public worship. We need both. And yet my hearing loss brought about a discouraging threat to both my desire and ability to participate on the Lord's Day.

At first church services were simply tiring, as making out the pastor's words required a lot of straining. The music became a little blurry, but since I already knew the tunes of the songs, I was still able to sing along. In just a few short years, however, church became a silent observation. The many songs and hymns I had come to love were reduced to words on a screen. I began to understand that losing the wonderful gift of music would be one of the biggest blows hearing loss would strike. Yes, the words could still be edifying, but silently reading the lyrics to a song is a much different experience from freely singing along with God's people when they have gathered together to worship Him.

There wasn't anything technology could do to help in the music department, but it certainly helped me glean more from the rest of the service. Pastors were willing to give me copies of any notes or manuscripts they had, and we were also able to try out a dictation software. This kind of software was still in its early development stages at the time, so it never ended up being a good solution. (Plus, it was hard not to laugh during a sermon when it typed the word *cheeses* instead of *Jesus*, among many other mistakes.) Eventually, the best solution was to bring a laptop to church and have someone type the sermon as best they could. That option was much better than not getting any of the sermon at all, and yet I longed to be able to just sit in my seat and listen, without my eyes having to be glued to a computer screen.

Unless you have the habit of sneaking out the back door during the last song, going to church also brings with it the inevitable opportunity (or obligation, depending on how you see it) to fellowship with brothers and sisters in Christ. In other words, corporate worship involves people—meeting visitors, initiating and maintaining friendships, after-service mingling, Bible study groups, and mentoring relationships. Before I lost my hearing, these were opportunities;

now, however, they were often dreaded obligations that required a lot of effort, willingness to be excluded, and a humble acceptance that a lot of interactions would simply be awkward. Admittedly, I was not always willing to joyfully accept those requirements and sometimes wasted no time getting out the door in order to free myself from the burden of communication.

Along with the communication barrier came the unwelcome feeling of being hindered. I wanted to use my God-given gifts for the good of the church, but some of my ideas and desires for doing so were not compatible with being deaf. At times, this left me both envious and discontent.

Me, Myself, and I

These were real challenges, and if I could sum them up, I would say that overall, they presented me with the perfect opportunity to turn inward. Rather than corporate worship being a time of joyful self-forgetfulness, it became a time of being extremely focused on myself. *I'm not getting much out of the singing time. I am so tired of looking at a dumb computer screen. I don't think so-and-so really understands me. I wish I could reach out to that younger woman, but I'm afraid communication would be too awkward. I'm definitely not sticking around after the service today.* Self-pity. Self-focused motives for worship. Insecurity. Together, these are a recipe for a life of miserable and fruitless corporate worship.

Being deaf may be a unique circumstance, but it is by no means the *only* circumstance that would threaten the joy and purity of gathering with God's people. The women in any given church are walking through a wide spectrum of challenges—all of which could tempt the sinful flesh to make Sunday a day of isolation, resentment, and a hardened heart toward both God and others. I can think of several examples from my own church. There are divorced women who might feel excluded or misunderstood, single women who long to worship alongside a husband, and tired mothers of toddlers who get only bits and pieces of the sermon. There are families of seminary students from other countries who may get frustrated with their lack of English expertise. There are mothers of children with special needs who perhaps dread going to church because it is exhausting and sometimes embarrassing. There are chronically ill women who suffer often in pain and weakness. There are women with rebellious adult children who face the weekly challenge of praising the Father and rejoicing with the sister whose children are walking faithfully with the Lord.

In all these situations—and many, many more—church can become a place where we fix our eyes on self—and particularly what we desire and do not have—instead of coming to God in worshipful gratitude or extending a word of encouragement to a sister. We are reminded of what our health is not, what our children are not, what our finances are not, what our parenting is not, what our marriage is not, what our holiness is not, what our social skills are not, and what our gifts are not. These reminders can be a perfect breeding ground for the sins of envy, covetousness, discontent, resentment, pride, and others. And when these sins rear their ugly heads, we become even more frustrated, because church becomes not only a place of sorrow but a place that exposes our sin. We know that we are called to worship with God's people. We know that we are called to love God's people. We know that we are called to serve God's people. But the fact is, *it's easier to spend three secluded hours at a coffee shop with a Bible, a prayer journal, and a Christian biography.*

There is nothing inherently wrong with a solitary trip to a coffee shop in pursuit of spiritual growth—or simply to enjoy a good cup of coffee in silence, for that matter. When life gets overwhelming, confusing, or painful, we are likely to crave those times alone. We can read our favorite passages of Scripture, pour out our hearts to a listening God, and read or listen to a sermon on the topic we think will be most relevant and helpful.

God can and does meet us in those times of private worship. But we must be aware that the Devil will try to make us think we can thrive spiritually on our own. He will pester us with the lie that if gathering with the body of Christ is painful, exhausting, or complicated; if it provokes us to sinful thoughts and attitudes—then we ought to just stay away. Our individualistic, live-streaming culture has taught us how to do this.

But God has not called us to live—or suffer—in isolation. He has made us to be part of a body with many members, of which Christ is the head (Rom. 12:5). And these members gather together to love and worship God, and love and serve one another: "And let us consider one another in order to stir up love and good works, not forsaking the assembling of ourselves together, as is the manner of some, but exhorting one another, and so much the more as you see the Day approaching" (Heb. 10:24–25).

This "one another" and "together" aspect of the Christian life is crucial for us to remember as we seek to be women who laugh at the days to come. The very truths that embolden us to laugh are also the truths that remind us we should not be laughing alone. If God is my Father, then I am part of a family—a family that regularly gathers together for worship. Within that family I have many sisters, and God has providentially placed *specific* sisters in my local church, with whom I can build unique relationships.

Not only do we share the same sovereign Father, but we also share the same elder Brother, whose perfect example we are encouraging one another to imitate. And it is this same elder Brother to whom we are both intimately united, as His Spirit indwells us and conforms us to His image.

As members of Christ's body, we each have a role. We do not all have the same role, and our roles may change as we go through different seasons of life. But what we do have in common is the fact that in order to fulfill our role we must purposefully *participate*. In the body of Christ, no one is called to be an idle spectator. Yes, our unique circumstances and particular stage of life play a part in what our participation looks like, but they do not *keep us* from participation.

The goal, then, is not to become independent, self-reliant women who are finding the strength to laugh behind closed doors. Rather, we lay down our pride and acknowledge the way God has created His people to thrive—together. And one of the primary places this togetherness takes place is in the local church on Sunday mornings, where imperfect people living in an imperfect world gather together to worship a perfect Father in hope of a perfect world to come.

In this chapter, I would like to look at three different aspects of participation in the body of Christ. When ongoing difficulties and future uncertainties overwhelm us, we will likely be tempted to fix our eyes on self and sit quietly (and perhaps bitterly) on the sidelines. But when the precious truths of the gospel invade our thinking, we will know that isolation is a miserable dead-end street in the Christian life. And thus, by the grace of God, we will refuse to let our circumstances keep us in seclusion. Rather, as we pursue a life of "together" laughter, we will *worship* to grow in grace, *walk* with the body of Christ, and *work* as a steward of our gifts.

We Worship

Growing in Grace

As I will note below, there are many ways Scripture commands us to live toward one another in the body of Christ. But before sinful people of all different backgrounds, opinions, vocations, incomes, needs, weaknesses, strengths, and preferences can obey those commands toward others, there needs to be a common denominator. In the body of Christ that common denominator is, of course, God. A diverse group of people are united in one body because they worship one God. When Paul exhorted the Ephesians to walk together in love and unity, he reminded them, "There is one body and one Spirit, just as you were called in one hope of your calling; one Lord, one faith, one baptism; one God and Father of all, who is above all, and through all, and in you all" (Eph. 4:4–6).

Our participation in the body of Christ begins with the truth that there is one holy, Creator God who is worthy of our worship. Before God saved us and brought us into His family, we were dead in our sins and blind to the truth, worshiping the creature instead of the Creator (Rom. 1:25). The body of Christ is a group of people whose eyes have been opened to the reality of who God is and what He has done for them. Because they have been united to Christ and His Spirit dwells within them, they are now able to humbly and corporately bow the knee and declare that He alone is holy, holy, holy. They are commanded and enabled to serve and love one another because they are commanded and enabled to love, serve, and worship one God.

My participation in the body of Christ is not primarily for myself, and it is not even primarily for my brothers and sisters in Christ. My participation in the body of Christ is primarily a declaration that I love, obey, and worship God. My life can declare this in many ways throughout the week, but God has set aside one day in particular on which He desires His people to gather together in worship. When I commit myself to a local church and make the effort to show up every Sunday to sit under the preaching of the word, participate in corporate prayer and praise, and partake of the Lord's Supper, I gain a weekly opportunity to correct my human-centered (i.e., me-centered) thinking and be reminded that my aim is to build my life around God and not self.

When the sorrow and sighing of life is great, it is easy to start making myself the center of the universe and resist the things I don't feel like doing. But when I walk through the doors of the church on Sunday morning, I come face-to-face with a multitude of individuals who are willingly gathering together to declare, "It is our joy to be a part of the body of Christ, and we are here to worship the God who has united us to each other and Himself."

Can I worship Him alone in my room as I read His word? Yes. Can I worship Him as I sing hymns in my car? Yes. Can I worship Him with my small group as we gather together to pray? Yes—and these are all good things. But there is something unique about corporate worship on Sunday in a local, biblical church, and we should be expectant for Him to meet with us there in a special way.

If God had simply commanded us in His word not to forsake the assembling of ourselves for the purpose of corporate worship and to do so by creating organized local churches characterized by godly leadership, sound preaching, and faithful administration of the sacraments, that alone would be reason enough to show up on Sunday—to gather in corporate worship simply because He tells us to and is worthy of that worship. And yet, loving Father that He is,

He has ordained for public worship to be a primary means of grace in our lives, which means that our commitment to it is for His glory, but also for our good and growth. When we choose to attend corporate worship, not only are we declaring "God is holy and worthy" but also "I am *not* holy and worthy. I am a needy sinner, and I have come expectant that God will use this time to strengthen my soul and make me more like Him."

Being Equipped

Seasons of difficulty or suffering will often result in a growing sweetness in our relationship with God. Our personal prayer times may grow more intense and intimate, and certain passages of Scripture we read and study during private devotions may minister to us in a greater way than they ever have before. Some passages of Scripture still remind me of when I was walking through hearing loss because God used them to specially encourage and strengthen me during that time. There is a reason why we refer to "the school of suffering"—the hardships of life teach and sanctify us like nothing else, and we certainly ought to be thankful for that.

And yet it is possible for us to begin thinking only about that *one* thing, the one area we are struggling in—be it singleness, motherhood, disease, a difficult relationship, the loss of a loved one, or some other trial. Every time we come to Scripture, we are drawn to passages that will encourage us in that area. Every time we search the Internet for a sermon to listen to, we look for something on that topic. It is right and good to expect that God will use our unique circumstances and trials to teach us about certain doctrines, sanctify us, and use us. But we also need to acknowledge that there are other areas in which we need to grow in our knowledge, understanding, and wisdom. When we devote ourselves to a biblical church and weekly sit under the preaching of the word, we are exposed to the "whole counsel of God," (Acts 20:27) as opposed to the counsel of our own choosing.

During the season I was expecting to be healed any minute, I remember going to church every Sunday very hopeful the pastor would have something to say that was relevant to suffering, healing, or the power of prayer. I wasn't going with a desire to grow in my knowledge of God's word as a whole; rather, I wanted to hear only something that would make me feel better about my unique circumstances. Not surprisingly, some Sundays I was disappointed.

The sober-minded woman who is learning to laugh at the days to come will have much encouragement and insight to offer regarding her specific area of suffering or struggle. Our unique life experiences are certainly one way God equips us to learn and then minister to others. But we also must keep in mind that there is much more to learn about God—His ways, His word, and His world—than what we learn through our own life experiences. Paul prayed that the Colossians would be "filled with the knowledge of His will in all wisdom and spiritual understanding" (Col. 1:9). Sitting under faithful preaching of God's word equips us to increasingly think and speak biblically about all areas of life—to not become "dull of hearing" and "unskilled in the word of righteousness" (Heb. 5:11, 13). Our goal is not to become women who know all about suffering through (fill in the blank), but to become women who feast on solid food and who "have their powers of discernment trained by constant practice to distinguish good from evil" (Heb. 5:14 ESV). Sometimes we will hear a sermon that is especially applicable to our current circumstances, and there is nothing wrong with the joy and appreciation we feel toward those times. But let us remember: "All Scripture is given by inspiration of God, and is profitable for doctrine, for reproof, for correction, for instruction in righteousness, that the man of God may be complete, thoroughly equipped for every good work" (2 Tim. 3:16–17).

Being Encouraged
We all love that feeling of being freshly encouraged after a coffee date with a like-minded friend, after lunch with a godly older woman who shares her wisdom, or after a weekend away with our husband when we can discuss goals and desires for the future and simply nurture the relationship. Often, those occasions of encouragement will

happen when we are able to temporarily step away from the daily grind and set aside our normal duties.

This past week I had the opportunity to sit down with an older woman from church who invited me over for lunch. For two hours we ate delicious Mexican food, shared our hearts with one another, and sipped tea. My heart was greatly refreshed by the time, and I was so grateful for this friend who was willing to both listen and speak the truth in love. I can't hire a babysitter in order to do that sort of thing every week, but I value the once-in-a-while opportunities to leave the dishes behind and have an uninterrupted heart-to-heart conversation.

Likewise, God gives us an opportunity every week to step away from the monotony of daily life so that we can be encouraged and built up as we attend and participate in corporate worship. Going to church doesn't make our problems go away—sometimes it causes us to think of them even more. But in that case, we can ask for and anticipate God's grace to make church a fruitful time of sanctification and edification rather than a time to harden our hearts and turn inward.

We are all coming from a wide range of experiences during the past week, but God knows exactly how to minister to each one of us personally through His Spirit. Just to be clear—it is not selfish for us to come to church with the hope that God will meet with and minister to us. There is a difference between coming to church with a "consumer" mind-set (looking only for how the church experience as a whole can meet our felt needs and cater to our preferences) and a sincere desire and expectancy to meet with and be changed by the living God as we participate in the service.

When we are careful to choose a biblical, Christ-centered church, corporate worship services become a feast for our weary minds and troubled hearts. Besides the preaching, there are several other elements of a corporate worship service that God uses to strengthen and build up weary saints.

There is something very wonderful about times of corporate singing, especially when the song lyrics are saturated with rich biblical truths. I am thankful my church chooses such songs because even though I long to hear and join in with the voices of God's people, I can still be encouraged when I purposefully read the lyrics.

The time of corporate prayer can also be an encouragement, not because the pastors are perfectly eloquent but because they are praying with thought and sincerity. The pastor does not rush corporate prayer to avoid listeners getting bored; rather, the pastor takes adequate time not only to bring specific needs before the Father but also to acknowledge who He is and what He has done for us through Christ.

Taking the Lord's Supper forces me to remember the gospel and that the grace to live a godly life does not come from myself, but from Christ, whose life nourishes mine and keeps me from falling away.

And last, we can simply be encouraged by looking around the room and acknowledging that everyone else chose to show up that morning. I am encouraged when I see the mother in front of me who patiently bears with her son with special needs. I am encouraged when I see the cheerful middle-school-aged girl making her way to her seat with her walker. I'm encouraged when I see Joanne, the ninety-year-old woman whose face glows with the joy of Christ and who refuses to miss a service if she doesn't have to.

Everyone's participation in the service that morning will look a little different, but as we come together for that hour and a half, we come to worship, love, and know the same God. And this is a precious foretaste of heaven, which is perhaps the most seldomly appreciated encouragement that awaits us on Sunday mornings. When the body of Christ gathers together, we get a hope-filled glimpse of that future day when people from every tongue, tribe, and nation will bow before the throne of heaven and worship God in unison. In that day, there will be absolutely nothing that hinders us from full and joy-filled participation, and it will go on for eternity. When that precious reality comes to mind during corporate worship, it encourages us to press on in a life of laughter.

We Walk with the Body of Christ

I greatly look forward to that day. But until then, the worship service comes to an end, and I am forced to face the dreaded fellowship hour. *Dreaded* may be a bit of an exaggeration, though I must confess, that is how I felt when we began attending a new church after moving to Michigan. Unfortunately, the threat of my deafness and facial paralysis being an embarrassment to myself or a burden to others did not pass away with my high school days. I was tempted (and still am some Sundays) to simply wander around the foyer or stand somewhere by myself flipping through a magazine I picked up at the resource counter. Was it edifying? Not really—but it took a lot less effort than joining a group conversation and a lot less courage than striking up a conversation with someone I didn't know.

On the way home from church, I usually regretted my failure to turn outward and make the effort to communicate with people, knowing it was an important part of participating in the body of Christ. God has designed the church to be a place where we come to meet not only with Him but also with others. The brothers and sisters in Christ with whom we commune every Sunday may be different from us in many ways, but our lives are (or at least should be) built around the same thing, the same Person. That simple fact should play a large part in my desire and willingness to get to know those people.

Furthermore, though we are united in one body to all Christians, there is something especially unique about the brothers and sisters we see every Sunday. When we devote ourselves to one local church, we commit ourselves to the specific people in that church. We serve a God who works in perfect providence. He does not place us in a specific country, state, city, and church with no purpose. He does not direct our steps only to a particular building but also to particular individuals. Recognizing this ought to make us value the opportunities we have each week to love, care for, and build relationships with the women we see week in and week out.

Why, then, does fellowship feel so complicated sometimes? Why is it so easy to avoid people or be content with surface-level conversation that never gets past a friendly "Hi, how are you?" or small talk about last week's weather? Perhaps there are many reasons, but I think one of the basic reasons is because fellowship involves people. And as we all know, people (including us) make life complicated. We make wrong assumptions, we miscommunicate, we get busy and forget about needs, we ramble on instead of listening, and we unintentionally exclude and misunderstand people. Fellowship is complicated because it involves people, and people are complicated because we are all sinners. And to top it all off, we are all walking through various difficulties, trials, and frustrations in life. We come to church as sisters, yes—but also as sinners and sufferers. And this makes our fellowship imperfect.

And yet, Scriptures makes it clear that the relationships ought to be there. We are called to a "one another" life within the body of Christ. We are commanded to

- love one another (John 13:34);
- give preference to one another (Rom. 12:10);
- receive one another (Rom. 15:7);
- admonish one another (Rom. 15:14);
- serve one another (Gal. 5:13);
- bear with one another (Eph. 4:2);
- be kind, tenderhearted, and forgiving toward one another (Eph. 4:32);
- comfort one another (1 Thess. 4:18);
- edify one another (1 Thess. 5:11);
- confess our sins to one another (James 5:16).

How can I obey these commands in Scripture if I am walking out the door every Sunday as soon as the benediction is given (or wandering around the foyer, for that matter)? Meaningful, edifying fellowship is not easy, and we all have various reasons why we would like to (or should be allowed to) avoid it at times. But without it, we will not learn to shift our constant gaze away from self and love people the way Christ's example has called us to. Learning to selflessly love imperfect people and participate in their lives is a lifelong learning process, but I would like to offer four simple suggestions for how we can do so as we seek to be women who laugh together.

Be present. In our technological day of social media and FaceTime, we are able to keep up with friends all over the world. I am thankful for ongoing friendships and contact I have with a handful of dear women from various seasons of life. But as much as I cherish those women, my efforts to maintain the friendships should not be keeping me from cultivating friendships in the church God has placed me in right now. Sure, the women in my current church may not "get" me like my old roommate does, but there is a reason why God has put those women in my life for this present season. When I take the time to invest in the women right in front of me, I can be expectant that He will providentially be at work in those relationships for my and others' good.

Be prayerful. When we are walking through something difficult and are tempted to keep to ourselves, we should ask God to use that specific difficulty to encourage or serve someone else. This mindset helps us to turn outward because rather than seeing our unique circumstance as a reason to avoid fellowship, we see it as a potential opportunity to help someone else. God has a way of using life's difficulties to bring about unexpected friendships and opportunities. Paul recognized that when God comforted him in affliction, one of the reasons was so that he could then be a comfort to someone else facing affliction: "Blessed be the God and Father of our Lord Jesus Christ, the Father of mercies and God of all comfort, who comforts us in all our tribulation, that we may be able to comfort those who are in any trouble, with the comfort with which we ourselves are comforted by God" (2 Cor. 1:3–4).

On another note, we ought to be prayerful in the friendships we already have. Everyone has their own hard situation—and many people have multiple ones. The past week may have been very difficult, but I am not the only one who comes to church in need of prayer. Remembering that is another way I can turn outward when I walk into church on Sunday morning. Asking our sisters how we can pray for them (and then actually taking the time to pray for them that week) is a very simple and yet effective way to show we care and can also be an open door for more intimate conversation that causes the friendship to deepen.

Be purposeful. We often tend to seek out relationships with women within our own age range or who are going through similar life experiences (e.g., parenting toddlers). Those friendships are wonderful and needed, but we would do well to expand our horizons and make it a point to seek out edifying fellowship with both older and younger women, as the Titus 2 model exhorts. We often hesitate to reach out for fear that our efforts may be rejected. And while it may be true that not every effort put forth will blossom into a growing friendship or mentor relationship, that should not keep us from making the first move. If we wait around for those relationships to come to us, they probably won't.

Be practical. By *practical* I mean *realistic.* A couple years ago, my family moved to Michigan so that my husband could attend seminary. Coming from a small church in Ohio, we were somewhat overwhelmed by the size of our new church. We were excited to get to know people and begin forming friendships, but it didn't take long for us to realize we couldn't possibly be close friends with everyone. I have found it helpful to keep this in mind in the days that have followed. While we can always be open to God bringing new friendships to us (and even hopeful that He will), it is okay to have those "go-to" women with whom we regularly fellowship at church. That is not to say that church fellowship ought to take the form of exclusive and unwelcoming cliques but that it is normal and even necessary to have regular conversation with certain women in order for friendships to flourish and move beyond small talk.

Another way to be realistic is to remember the vitally important truth that even the most wonderful friendships we form within the body of Christ are not meant to satisfy us in the same way that Christ is able to satisfy us. We would be wise to take note of how much we are affected by the interactions we have with others. If I come home on Sunday discouraged because a certain friendship isn't progressing the way I want it to or because I didn't get to talk to so-and-so, I probably need to examine my motives for those relationships and whether I am trying to fill a space that only Christ can fill.

We Work to Steward Our Gifts

When Jesus had only a short time left with His disciples before His crucifixion, He wanted to leave them with a beautiful example of serving others. As they gathered in the upper room to share the Passover meal, Jesus humbly knelt down and washed their dusty, dirty feet. He exhorted them, "If I then, your Lord and Teacher, have washed your feet, you also ought to wash one another's feet" (John 13:14). From our viewpoint, it would have made more sense for the disciples to be serving Jesus at that moment. His last hour was drawing near, and He knew it was going to be unthinkably agonizing. But the Son of Man had not come to be served—He had come to serve. That doesn't mean He gave no thought to His present and approaching suffering or that He never received the ministry of loving service from anyone else. But He was not so consumed by His own suffering that it caused Him to be blind to the needs of others.

Jesus left us this example not so that we could simply admire it, but so that we could imitate it, especially toward our brothers and sisters in Christ. Paul tells us to do good to all people, but "especially to those who are of the household of faith" (Gal. 6:10). As we participate in the body of Christ, we are not just building relationships with people; we are aiming to serve them by consistently using our time, abilities, and God-given gifts, both on Sunday morning and throughout the week.

Seasons of suffering as well as ongoing challenges and limitations may change how or to what extent we are able to serve others, but nowhere in Scripture do we get the idea that it is only for those who have all their ducks in order. To put it bluntly—we are not excused from serving God's people when life is hard. Remember, the book of 1 Peter is written to Christians who are likely facing either persecution or the potential for it in the near future. And yet Peter does not encourage them to turn inward and focus on their own individual needs. Rather, he writes, "And above all things have fervent love for one another, for 'love will cover a multitude of sins.' Be hospitable to one another without grumbling. As each one has received a gift, minister it to one another, as good stewards of the manifold grace of God" (1 Peter 4:8–10).

We are called to actively love the body of Christ, and to do so we must be careful stewards of the gifts, abilities, and time that God has given us. Stewards are assigned to manage and govern over something specific. They are concerned about and attentive to that which is within their sphere of responsibility—that which they have been given, not what they haven't been given. One of the traps we fall into when it comes to serving is dwelling on all the ways we have not been equipped and gifted to serve, while envying those who are able to serve in those ways.

I will be the first one to admit that my own participation in serving the body of Christ has at times been hindered because of discouragement and frustration over my limitations. As a steward of grace, I am to joyfully accept that which is given to me and use it to glorify God and do good to His people. But sometimes I am not content with the grace I have been given and wish I was able and equipped to serve the way so-and-so can. So I have a choice. I could continue to dwell on my limitations and in the meantime do very little serving at all. Or I could humbly acknowledge what time, resources, abilities, and gifts God has given me, and then pray and look for opportunities to serve others with them.

When my husband started leading the college and career group at church last year, I was discouraged by how my deafness was a hindrance to participating in the meetings, which mostly consist of group discussion. As much as I would love to help lead in that group, I have had to accept that God has not equipped me physically to thrive in that sort of role. It is the same reason I'm not signing up to teach a Sunday school class or lead the children's singing time.

Thankfully, there are many other ways to serve in the body of Christ, and it is my responsibility to say, "Okay, God, what *can* I do?" and when He shows me, go do it. I may not have enough space to host a large women's Bible study in my home, but I can regularly practice hospitality and invite one family at a time over for dinner. I may not be equipped physically to interact with a large group of children in the Backyard Bible Club outreach this summer, but I can offer to watch a friend's kids for a few hours. It wouldn't be very practical for me to lead a Bible study, but I can take the time to write and send encouraging cards to people.

We all have various life circumstances that make us feel discouraged, limited, frustrated, drained, or simply "different." When we intentionally look for ways to serve the body of Christ, we do not have to pretend those circumstances don't exist—they *do*. And while they may cause our participation to look different from someone else's, they should not be making us self-focused, envious, or discontent observers from the sideline. Rather, the very difficulties those limitations present us can serve as a needed reminder that we are participating in a body. The goal is not a bunch of independent individuals performing in the spotlight for their own glory, but a body "joined and knit together by what every joint supplies, according to the effective working by which every part does its share," in which Christ "causes growth of the body for the edifying of itself in love" (Eph. 4:16).

We worship together, we walk together, and we work together, under one Head—Christ. And as we gather as one body, we humbly proclaim with one voice, "to *Him* be glory in the church by Christ Jesus to all generations, forever and ever. Amen" (Eph. 3:21, emphasis added). This is the heart cry of a woman who laughs at the days to come alongside her sisters in Christ. Though the trials of earthly life entice her to gaze inward, by the grace of God she looks intently at her humble Savior and is compelled to press on in a life of faithful worship and selfless love.

Eleven

HER PROSPECT
The Heavenly Aim of a Pilgrim

Now I saw a new heaven and a new earth, for the first heaven and the first earth had passed away. Also there was no more sea. Then I, John, saw the holy city, New Jerusalem, coming down out of heaven from God, prepared as a bride adorned for her husband. And I heard a loud voice from heaven saying, "Behold, the tabernacle of God is with men, and He will dwell with them, and they shall be His people. God Himself will be with them and be their God. And God will wipe away every tear from their eyes; there shall be no more death, nor sorrow, nor crying. There shall be no more pain, for the former things have passed away."

—Revelation 21:1–4

It has been more than a year since I started writing this book, and within that time nothing drastic has happened. In the beginning stages of writing, I wondered if perhaps God had ordained some terrible trial to take place so that the truths I was writing about would be further driven home in my heart. Instead, both of my boys got through the winter with hardly any sickness. Food was on the table, friendships were formed and strengthened, and God once again proved faithful to my husband through another year of seminary.

Oh, there were smaller difficulties, to be sure. On many occasions I awoke in the middle of the night with nerve pain; parenting continued to be a monumental and sometimes discouraging task; our tired minivan gave way a few weeks ago; and the deafness I have come to be at peace with is still at times something I despise and grieve.

On the one hand, I'm still waiting for something big to happen—still fighting that tendency to assume that because life has been relatively comfortable for a while, there must be something incredibly painful up ahead. On the other hand, I find myself wondering when all those smaller things will stop happening. When will the car troubles cease? When will I completely overcome the challenges of being deaf? When will I feel like I am really thriving in my parenting?

This season of life has been filled with the enjoyment of good and perfect gifts from a kind and gracious Father. But it has also come with the growing realization that there will always be something unwanted, difficult, or imperfect. I am reminded of this even tonight as I find myself bothered by the newly discovered scratch on my dining table—a small thing, but nonetheless a perfect test for the homemaker who can't seem to go a week without something breaking or wearing out. This is the reality of life in a fallen world. Even the good is not perfect, and the beautiful is not without decay. Yes, life could take a turn for the worse next week or next year—and maybe it will. But even if it doesn't and this present season remains overall quite ordinary and peaceful, the hours, days, weeks, and months will still be speckled with circumstances and sorrows that remind me on what side of heaven I am currently living. In most of these cases, people won't be showing up on my doorstep with a hot meal and I won't need help from a professional biblical counselor. Most people will probably never even know the specifics of what minor or temporary trials and frustrations my family and I are walking through.

Either way, the sober truth remains: I am the clay, and my Father is the potter. I do not get to choose how I suffer in this life. This is the Christian's peculiar perspective on suffering.

We do not choose, but we do respond; in other words, we live—we make choices, we deliberately think about things, we allow certain attitudes, and we talk to friends and family about what is going on in life; we read books, we commune with God in prayer, we spend money, we choose how to spend our time, we foster or fight against sin, we listen to sermons, and we browse the Internet. In all these things and a hundred more, we speak to the world around us about our ultimate prospect in life: *What is my confident expectation? What am I looking ahead to? What reality constantly permeates my daily living?* Whether we are responding to days of prosperity, months of pain, or something in between, our conviction about what these earthly days amount to will be evident in the words we speak, the choices we make, and the things we think about.

The woman who laughs at the days to come possesses and increasingly cultivates a heavenly and eternal prospect. The big and small details of her daily life reflect a hope that looks far beyond earthly circumstances. With sober-minded intention, she sets the gaze of her mind on heavenly realities, both present and future. Because she knows and believes the present gospel realities about who she is, whose she is, and where she is going, she is also able to take great delight in future realities, unseen as they are. She does not try to escape her present circumstances or wish them away. Rather, she courageously stares her circumstances in the face and declares the truths that dominate them. Following in the footsteps of her obedient Savior, she embraces every trial her Father ordains—not because it is easy, but because she has a real joy set before her. She knows that every passing day is getting her closer to that final joy, and therefore she laughs.

The Believer's Present Privileges

When eternal glory is the lens through which we look at present suffering, we laugh in the face of life's trials and frustrations, confidently looking ahead to the day we will be released from our weariness and ushered into a tearless eternity.

But does our laughter have nothing but heaven in view? Is there nothing to laugh about as we consider what the coming days and months on earth may hold? Are we laughing only because we hope for heaven?

I hope the chapters leading up to this one have given a clear answer to these questions: *no, we are not laughing in anticipation of heaven only.* The realities of the gospel give us reason to expect that our earthly days will include manifold joys, comforts, and blessings, though they may simultaneously be filled with painful trials. We can laugh because we know that present or approaching suffering is ordained by a Father who will use it for our highest good. We can laugh because we look forward to the joy of growing in godliness, as we keep our eyes on the perfect example of Christ and expect an abundant supply of grace to better understand His character and imitate it. We can laugh because we know we are intimately united to Christ by His Spirit, and because of that union, the Spirit is at work in us daily to make us more like Him.

We can laugh because we trust that when painful circumstances drive us to fervently pour out our hearts to God in prayer, He will not turn His face away, but will hear and comfort us with His word. And we can laugh because we have been given the present joy of being part of the local church and the body of Christ. Though the sermons and relationships may not be perfect, we press on in our conviction that a life of worship, walking, and working together is a means God uses to sustain and strengthen His beloved children.

Every person on earth has trials of some kind at one point or another, simply because we live in a fallen world of cancer, car trouble, and relational conflict. But there is a real and particular earthly comfort that is offered to and experienced only by believers. Heaven is a happy reality and final reward, but we do not go through our earthly days without many benefits and privileges—even in the midst of suffering—which are completely unknown to those without Christ. Charles Spurgeon said it well:

> We are, my brothers and sisters, married unto Christ; and shall our great Bridegroom permit His spouse to linger in constant grief? Our hearts are knit unto Him—we are members of His body, of His flesh, and of His bones, and though for a while we may suffer as our head once suffered, yet we are even now blessed with heavenly blessings in Him. Shall our head reign in heaven, and shall we have a hell upon earth? God forbid! The joyful triumph of our exalted head is in a measure shared by us,

even in this vale of tears. We have the earnest of our inheritance in the comforts of the Spirit which are neither few nor small.[1]

The believer's present experience is reason enough to laugh at the earthly days to come. And yet this happy truth does not disregard the reality that we do suffer greatly while on earth. The comforting realities of the gospel propel us to persevere, but they do not promise earthly prosperity, at least not as the world defines prosperity. Indeed, to be a Christian is to be strengthened, sanctified, comforted, and protected; but it is not to be healed from every sickness, released from every financial woe, or kept from all forms of disappointment, loss, and conflict. The blessings and privileges of the Christian life are real and many, but we must acknowledge that the pains and sufferings of the Christian life are real and many as well. Paul even goes as far as to say that God doesn't just allow suffering—He *grants* it, as though it were a gift: "For to you it has been granted on behalf of Christ, not only to believe in Him, but also to suffer for His sake" (Phil. 1:29). Suffering is not just normal for the believer, but a normal privilege.

A Higher Hope

Yes, we can confidently laugh at the earthly days to come and expect that whatever comes our way, God will get us through it. But there is indeed more to our laughter. We do not laugh only because God will get us through it, but because *God will get us home*.

I am reminded of 1 Corinthians 15:19. Paul wants the Corinthians to understand and believe the fact that Christ did not stay in the grave. He triumphantly rose from the dead, ascended into heaven, and sat down at the right hand of the Father. This is extremely good news that has significant implications for how the Corinthians will think and live. If Christ didn't rise from the dead, then His death

---

1. Charles H. Spurgeon, "Alas for Us, If Thou Wert All, and Nought Beyond, O Earth," in *The Metropolitan Tabernacle Pulpit* (Pasadena, Tex.: Pilgrim Publications, 1976), 10:182.

was not an effective atonement for sin and the Corinthians are thus not reconciled with the holy God. He is not their Father but rather a judge whose holy wrath is on them. If Christ did not rise, they are not united to Him and their lives are not under the sanctifying and preserving power of His Spirit. If Christ did not rise, they have been deceived and have put their faith in a complete sham. Every difficulty they have cheerfully embraced, every chastisement they have humbly submitted to, and every sorrow in which they have sought the comfort of Christ—if Christ did not rise, it was entirely in vain.

Paul sums it up well: "If in this life only we have hope in Christ, we are of all men the most pitiable" (1 Cor. 15:19). If there is nothing more to look forward to than a short earthly life in a fallen world, then believers are not of all men the most privileged, but of all men the most pitiable.

If for this life only we laugh at the days to come, we are of all women the most pitiable. Why? Because a life of laughter compels us to expect and embrace trials, not eliminate or escape them. But if the gospel is not true, if Christ has not been raised, and thus we will not be raised, "Let us eat and drink, for tomorrow we die!" (1 Cor. 15:32). In other words, if there is no hope for anything beyond this short earthly life, then we might as well stop embracing the trials of life and instead seek every possible earthly pleasure, since we are just going to die in the end anyway. If our suffering is not working for us the eternal joy of glorification, why voluntarily accept the Christian responsibility to suffer well?

And the Christian does have that responsibility. Though our benefits in suffering are many, those benefits also come with responsibilities, the chief of those being to glorify God. And the only way we can glorify God through the pain and weariness of life is if we are responding, thinking, speaking, and doing in a way that is in accordance with His word. Those without Christ may respond to the difficulties of life with selfishness, anger, laziness, gluttony, covetousness, and bitterness. They have no desire to be made holy, no loving Father urging them to keep their eyes on the prize, no suffering Savior they want to know more intimately. There is no crown, no joy set before them. Therefore, though they are not able to avoid much of their suffering, they can at least try to counter it by gratifying their flesh with constant pleasure, unrestrained emotions, and the active pursuit of anything that would make life feel easier.

This is not so for the believer—not because selfless, holy, biblical living in a fallen world is easy but because their selfless, holy, biblical living has an eternal end that is far more pleasurable and far more glorious than even the joy they experience from it this side of heaven. They are genuinely comforted by the Father's love now; they are genuinely enjoying the peaceful fruit of righteousness and intimate union with Christ now. But the reason they can enjoy the comforts of the gospel presently is the same reason they will not *merely* enjoy the comforts of the gospel presently. Because the gospel is true, not only do they rejoice in the love of their sovereign Father here but they rejoice in the reality that one day they will actually be in His presence, knowing His love fully.

At the end of the day, what is the believer's gaze fixed on? Her gaze is fixed on an eternal weight of glory beyond all comparison. As she looks on her unseen future in heaven, she can say along with Paul that her earthly afflictions are "light" and "but for a moment" (2 Cor. 4:17). She is able to describe her afflictions in that way not because she is comparing them to the present benefits of being a believer but because she is comparing them to what those present benefits are leading to—her final, perfect, and complete glorification in heaven.

Paul's words are worth repeating: "For we know that the whole creation groans and labors with birth pangs together until now. Not only that, but we also who have the firstfruits of the Spirit, even we ourselves groan within ourselves, eagerly waiting for the adoption, the redemption of our body" (Rom. 8:22–23). Even we ourselves who have the firstfruits of the Spirit—and all the benefits therein—are groaning. This is not a miserable groaning, but a hope-filled groaning. Paul describes this groaning elsewhere: "For we who are in this tent groan, being burdened, not because we want to be unclothed, but further clothed, that mortality may be swallowed up by life"

(2 Cor. 5:4). What burden is weighing on Paul? Perhaps the greatness of his affliction is part of his burden, but more than that, he is burdened with longing for heaven. Mark A. Seifrid comments, "The promise of the dwelling from heaven, the life of the resurrection, weighs upon him, burdening his present life with unstillable longing and restlessness. The hope of the resurrection is no narcotic that leaves its possessors passive, listless, and dormant. On the contrary, it makes them restless pilgrims."[2]

Restless pilgrims. We are laughing at the days to come, and in that laughter, there is holy longing; a longing for this weary pilgrimage to be finished that we might finally be home and with Christ. Paul goes on to say, "For we were saved in this hope, but hope that is seen is not hope; for why does one still hope for what he sees? But if we hope for what we do not see, we eagerly wait for it with perseverance" (Rom. 8:24–25). We were saved *in hope*. In other words, our salvation does not completely and perfectly satisfy us here on earth. Rather, it gives us a mere foretaste—a genuinely sweet and comforting foretaste, to be sure—that compels our hearts to long for the day when we will be able to taste it fully. If there is no restless longing for more, if all our rejoicing is in the present sweetness of salvation, we have failed to understand the glory of the gospel.

We must not miss this. We have been given a "now and not yet" salvation. We spend a lot of time talking, thinking, reading, debating, and praying about the "now," but for some reason the "not yet" and the hope we ought to have for it get neglected. We daily enjoy the "now," but we must frequently envision and meditate on the "not yet" because the "now" is meaningless without it.

Getting Our Hopes Up

I think pregnancy is one of the best real-life illustrations we have of gospel hope. It shows us both the necessity of envisioning the "not yet" and the absurdity of neglecting it. When I was pregnant with

---

2. Mark A. Seifrid, *The Second Letter to the Corinthians*, ed. D. A. Carson, Pillar New Testament Commentary (Grand Rapids: Eerdmans, 2014), 228.

my first son, I had a friend who was also due with her first baby just a couple days before me. When her bump started showing before mine, I was both envious of her visible evidence and anxious to know if there was really a baby growing inside me. Then she got her first ultrasound and had even more visible assurance. Because we had paid a fairly large amount for an excellent midwife, we did not have the extra cash for ultrasounds throughout the pregnancy. Though I was showing a bit by then and Nick had heard our son's heartbeat, I longed to be able to *see* the baby. Was he really there? Was he growing and developing as he was supposed to?

By the fourth month, I was no longer wondering if there was a baby growing inside me—that much was obvious. The question became, Will the baby make it? Will the baby make it out of me—alive? At that point, I needed more than faith. It was one thing to believe the baby existed, and yet another thing to hope that I would one day hold that newborn baby in my arms. In faith I believed the baby was there, but in hope I needed to attend my baby showers, decorate the nursery, and install the car seat.

Now imagine if by the end of the eighth month my belly was bulging and I had felt the baby move daily. What if at that point I had done none of the things mentioned above? What if someone had asked me the baby's name and I answered, "I'm not sure; we haven't really thought about it much." Or what if someone had asked me if I was nervous and excited, and I casually replied, "I'm trying not to think about the labor and delivery too much—I don't want to get my hopes up that the baby will make it out okay." I would certainly get some raised eyebrows and looks of confusion.

Pregnant women do not merely believe they are pregnant—they get their hopes up. And for the next nine months they talk and live and think in such a way that shows they are confidently expecting that one day soon they will be holding a precious baby in their arms. The pregnancy isn't easy. There is nausea, poor sleep, exhaustion, and many other discomforts. What drives them on? Hope—of sweet relief and final reward.

The analogy must end there because, as we know, there are earthly pregnancies that do not end the way they are supposed to. Less than a year after my first son was born, plump and healthy, I heard the news that a friend had given birth to a stillborn baby boy. She had walked out her pregnancy with joyful, active hope, but in the end those hopes were dashed to pieces and met with profound grief. What she confidently expected never came. But this is never the sad reality of the believer.

We live in the happy reality that our hope of one day being with Christ in heaven will not prove vain. On that last day, when the trumpet sounds and the Lord descends, our hope will not be pitiable but proven. The things we read about but didn't quite know how to envision—we will suddenly see and hear them, know and experience them.

It is one thing to believe that all this will one day come to pass but yet another thing to live with steadfast *hope* that it will come to pass. The woman who laughs at the days to come does not simply believe that heaven is real—she expects to be there someday. And that expectation is not something that randomly comes to mind once in a while; rather, her future glorification becomes a lens through which she is constantly looking—when she reads her Bible, when she prays, when she receives bad news, when she meets with God's people, and when she is overwhelmed with caring for her family. As she reads God's word, she counts herself among the elect pilgrims, and there discovers many truths, exhortations, and promises that will help to press her onward toward her heavenly goal. When she meets with painful circumstances, she is still looking through that lens, seeing her trials as necessary stepping-stones that will bring her one pace closer to the destination she is aiming for. And in all her looking, there is *longing*, for she is not looking at an empty heaven, but she is looking unto Jesus, who has gone there before her and has prepared a place for her. She is a restless pilgrim and cannot escape the blessed reality that one day she will be home.

A few years ago I read a memoir of Mary Winslow, the mother of Octavius Winslow, a prominent nineteenth-century preacher in

England and America. The book is mostly made up of letters she wrote to her family and friends, and her words show much about what kind of woman she was. When Mary was forty-one years old, she embarked on a ship to New York with her ten children. Her husband had experienced significant financial disaster after retiring from the army, and America was a place that offered them an opportunity to rebuild and move on. She and her children would make the trip first, and her husband would arrive on another ship a few months later. But things did not go as planned. Soon after they arrived in America, Mary's infant daughter grew sick and died. Before she even had a chance to bury her, she received word from overseas that her husband had also passed away. She was now a widow with nine children, alone in a strange land.[3]

Though her grief was overwhelming, Mary did not crumble. Her Father mightily sustained her, and her letters reflect a woman who treasured the gospel, loved her Savior, and grew in godliness. When I read her letters, it became obvious that the reason Mary was able to persevere through a life of such hardship was because she increasingly had her sights set on her heavenly home. An intimate relationship with Christ did prove to be a sweet refuge to her in the midst of her earthly pain, but she knew there was more to come. She was a restless pilgrim and knew that one day her longing for heaven would be realized. In one letter to a friend she wrote,

> Oh, let us not lose sight of heaven for a moment. How prone we are to allow our minds and hearts (treacherous hearts!) to become entangled with the baubles of a dying world.... Heaven is our home—our happy home. We are but strangers and pilgrims here. Try and realise it. Let us keep ourselves ready to enter with Him to the marriage supper of the Lamb. A little while, and we shall see Him, not as the "Man of sorrows," but the "King in His beauty." Shall we not know Him the moment we get there? Shall we not recognise that blessed countenance, which so often cheered and encouraged us when cast down?

3. Octavius Winslow, ed., *Life in Jesus: A Memoir of Mary Winslow* (Grand Rapids: Reformation Heritage Books, 2013), 65–70.

Dear friend, we shall. Then let us fight against earth and all its false attractions, for it passeth away. Let us keep close to Christ.[4]

Is this not the very same prospect we see in Scripture? The Epistles are bursting with a hope-filled heavenly prospect that is hard to miss in even a brief run-through. Just as in Mary's letters, it is obvious that all of Paul's, Peter's, and John's concerns regarding the present life of the Christian and the church as a whole were aiming toward one thing: Christ's return, creation's renewal, and the believer's glorification. Every command the Holy Spirit inspired, every encouragement from the gospel, every correction, every affirmation, every explanation of God's character, every exhortation—in all these things, the end goal was not a happy Christian life on earth, but a coming, eternal life with Christ in heaven. The reality of it weighed on these men. Their aim was not simply to teach people what to believe and how to live but to get it deep into their consciences that their doctrine and daily life were preparing them for the day when their faith would be turned to sight.

The gospel we believe by faith now will in that day become sight. We will see the Father's open arms and approving smile, and we will bow before the nail-scarred hands of Christ. The holiness that we pursue now will in that day be perfected, and as we gaze on the perfect holiness of Christ, "we shall be like Him, for we shall see Him as He is" (1 John 3:2).

This is the same reason Peter exhorted his suffering readers to rejoice in the midst of their trials with "joy inexpressible and full of glory" (1 Peter 1:8). The purpose of their rejoicing was not to make them a band of happy-go-lucky believers who pretended their pain was less than it really was. They weren't rejoicing in the pain—they were rejoicing in their prospect, the day when they would see face-to-face the Savior in whom they believed and whom they loved.

---

4. Winslow, *Life in Jesus,* 357–58.

Believing sound doctrine is not an end in itself. Holy living is not an end in itself. Rejoicing in trials is not an end in itself. The only reason we aim for these things is because we are ultimately aiming for heaven. If we detach these things from that end, they immediately lose their luster and even their meaning.

If for this life only we laugh at the days to come, we are of all women the most pitiable. So then, how do we do otherwise? How do we become women whose laughter is deeply rooted in a longing for and expectation of eternity with Christ? How do we laugh *here*, but fix our gaze on things *there*? This is no easy task in a culture of instant gratification, ever-present distraction, and books galore that promise the good life now.

Unfortunately, there is no quick-fix formula to becoming a heavenly-minded, hope-filled woman. Just as in other areas of sanctification, God works in us slowly, patiently conforming us to Christ. There may be seasons in which we especially find ourselves learning to look at life through the lens of heavenly hope. In other seasons, perhaps when we begin to feel comfortable and the things that once pained us become mundane and normal, we may find ourselves easily forgetting about heavenly realities—until it suddenly dawns on us that we are not as satisfied as we would like to be, but instead quite weary. We will likely experience both, but what we must remember is that the laughter-filled life that keeps a steady gaze on eternity is one we must never stop cultivating.

Paul sums it up well in a passage that has greatly encouraged believers through the ages: "So we do not lose heart. Though our outer self is wasting away, our inner self is being renewed day by day. For this light momentary affliction is preparing for us an eternal weight of glory beyond all comparison, as we look not to the things that are seen but to the things that are unseen. For the things that are seen are transient, but the things that are unseen are eternal" (2 Cor. 4:16–18 ESV).

Why did Paul's trial-filled life not cause him to lose heart? Because even though Paul's physical body was growing weaker, there was something *daily* going on inside him that caused him to keep running the race, to keep looking unto Jesus, to keep fighting the good fight. Day by day, hour by hour, the Holy Spirit was renewing Paul, giving him fresh joy in the gospel, fresh trust in God, and fresh hope for heaven. John Piper explains it well:

> The car of your hope and strength and joy is not meant to run on yesterday's gas. The metabolism of your spiritual renewal is not meant to run on yesterday's meal. The relief from your spiritual medicine does not come from yesterday's dosage. The text says "day by day" the renewal comes! There are no spiritual booster shots that last for ten years. There are no meals designed by God to carry you for a year.[5]

How thankful we should be that the Holy Spirit is daily at work in the children of God to provide them with fresh nourishment! He does allow us to become painfully aware of when our spiritual gas tank is running on empty. But He does not expect us to fill it up ourselves. He comes to us daily in a hundred ways we often don't even recognize and gives us the grace we need to keep running, to keep laughing.

We are renewed day by day—but not as puppets. As God works in us to will and to do for His good pleasure, we work out our own salvation (Phil. 2:12–13). If we will be found laughing, we will not be found idle. And with this thought we come full circle, remembering Peter's exhortation to a band of suffering saints: "Therefore gird up the loins of your mind, be sober, and rest your hope fully upon the grace that is to be brought to you at the revelation of Jesus Christ" (1 Peter 1:13).

A woman who laughs—who sets her hope on the grace that is to be brought to her—is a woman who thinks. And a woman who thinks soundly will be a woman who lives soundly. She believes the gospel and thinks rightly about it, and her resulting godly life is evidence of that. She does this in the day of prosperity, and she does this

---

5. John Piper, "The Glory of God in the Sight of Eternity," Sermons, Desiring God, July 26, 2013, https://www.desiringgod.org/messages/the-glory-of-god-in-the-sight-of-eternity.

in the day of suffering. She does not walk in holiness perfectly, but because the Spirit is daily at work in her and she keeps a close guard on her mind, she walks in holiness increasingly.

She is aware that she must remind herself often of the comforting truths of the gospel. They are truths to be not only known and believed but studied and pondered. And the more she ponders them, the more she comes to understand how the realities of the gospel are present realities that transform the way she is responding to earthly circumstances. Little by little she discovers more of what it means to be adopted by a sovereign Father who does not keep her from difficulty, but always uses it for her highest good. Year by year she comes to better understand what it means to humbly follow in the footsteps of her sinless Savior and draw grace from her unbreakable union with Him.

She is a woman who treasures truth, and therefore she is a woman who is able to laugh at the days to come. But at the end of the day, there is a truth that overshadows them all, and a truth that keeps her laughing: the things that are seen are transient, but the things that are unseen are eternal. *She is not yet home.*

Dear sisters, if we are to go on laughing, let us treasure the truth that we are pilgrims who tomorrow will be one day closer to the unseen things of eternity that far outweigh both the intensity of our present pain and the sweetness of our present salvation. Our Father, God Himself, will welcome us with open arms, and we will experience His love in a way we cannot fathom here. Our husband, the risen and exalted Christ, will joyfully meet us at the marriage supper. The intimate union we share with Him even now will be felt, understood, and cherished as it never could be here, where we see only dimly. Every sigh will be of happy relief. Every tear will be only for joy. And we shall laugh once more, for we shall be safely home. Perhaps Mary Winslow has captured it best:

> Oh, the joy of soon being with Jesus! Heaven is very near. The eternal world is all around us. Oh to realise this continually! We do not dwell sufficiently on these glorious realities; we do not bring them home to ourselves. We are either too much

engaged with earthly things, or are looking more within the dark recesses of our hearts, than to the glory that awaits us, and into the possession of which we might be any moment introduced.[6]

---

6. Winslow, *Life in Jesus*, 366.

SCRIPTURE INDEX